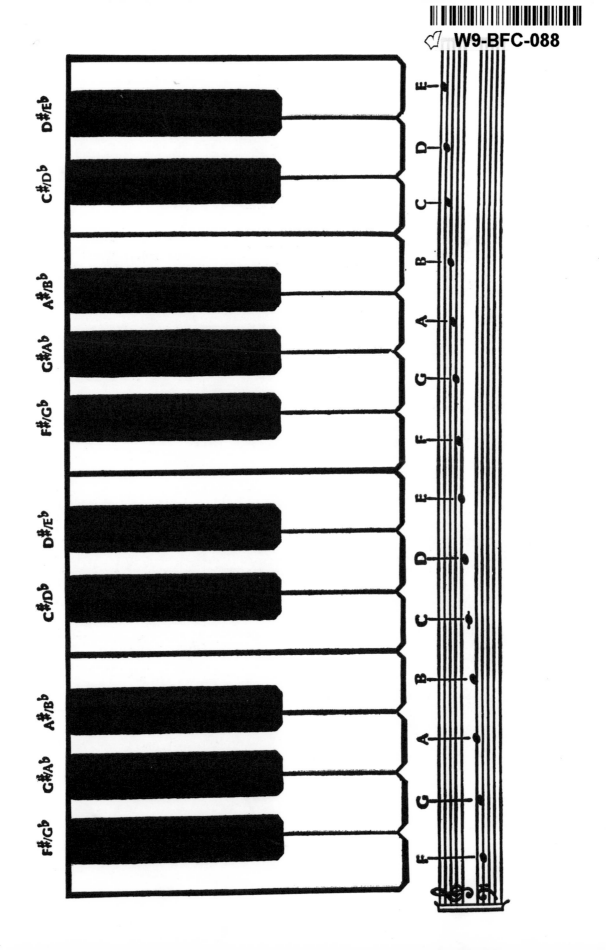

THE Music CONNECTION

PROGRAM AUTHORS

Jane Beethoven
Dulce Bohn
Patricia Shehan Campbell
Carmen E. Culp
Jennifer Davidson
Lawrence Eisman
Sandra Longoria Glover
Charlotte Hayes

Martha Hilley
Mary E. Hoffman
Hunter March
Bill McCloud
Marvelene Moore
Catherine Nadon-Gabrion
Mary Palmer
Carmino Ravosa

Mary Louise Reilly
Will Schmid
Carol Scott-Kassner
Jean Sinor
Sandra Stauffer
Judith Thomas

RECORDING PRODUCERS

Darrell Bledsoe
Jeanine Levenson

J. Douglas Pummill
Buryl Red, Executive Producer

Linda Twine
Ted Wilson

SILVER BURDETT GINN

PARSIPPANY, NJ   NEEDHAM, MA

Atlanta, GA   Deerfield, IL   Irving, TX   San Jose, CA

ISBN 0-382-26186-0

C · O · N · T

CONCEPTS................2

Introduction – Style		4
Unit 1	Rhythm	7
2	Melody	24
3	Harmony	34
4	Tone Color	42
5	Form	60
6	Style	70
7	Musical Interaction	84
8	Rhythm	92
9	Melody	102
10	Harmony	110
11	Style	118

THEMES...............130

Unit 1	The Turn of the Century	132
2	Bands Around the World	144
3	Dance—A World Tradition	156
4	Preparation for Performance	170
5	Careers in Music	184
6	Songs for Our Country	188
7	Music for the Holidays	198
8	Theme Musical	220
9	Performance Musical	230

·E·N·T·S

READING 254

Unit 1	Review	256
2	Dotted Patterns	263
3	I - IV - V$_7$ Chords	271
4	Cut Time	282
5	Parallel Thirds	288
6	Introducing *si*	291
7	Introducing *fi*	297
8	Introducing *ta*	310

REFERENCE BANK

Playing the Guitar	316
Playing the Recorder	322
Playing the Autoharp	326
Sound Bank	330
Glossary	336
Classified Index	338
Song Index	344
Acknowledgments	346
Picture Credits	346

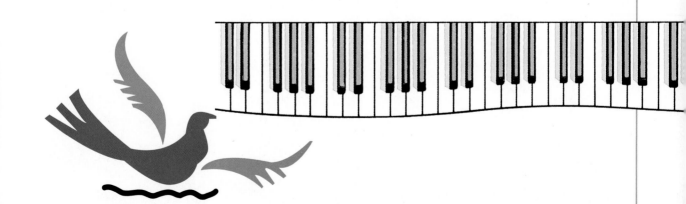

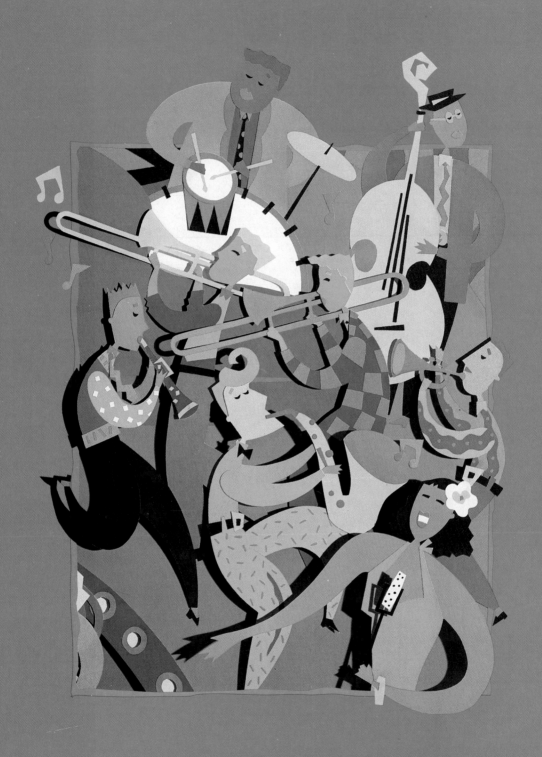

CONCEPTS

Prepare yourself—you are about to take
a musical trip around the world!

✳

You will soon realize that no matter where you go,
music is made up of these elements—
rhythm, melody, harmony,
form, style,
and tone color.

✳

Every culture that you explore will treat
these elements in various ways.
Because of this, every country's music
is different, much like its language and customs.

✳

So keep your eyes, ears, and mind open—
you will get a taste of the many
musical flavors of the world.

section

1

A Time to Unite

In 1985, many countries in Africa were in desperate need of help. Severe droughts had destroyed nearly all crops and livestock, and millions of people were facing critical shortages of food, water, and medical supplies.

A group of musicians decided to take action. Michael Jackson and Lionel Richie wrote the song "We Are the World," and together with the help of other jazz, country, and rock musicians, joined to form United Support of Artists for Africa (USA for Africa). Over $60 million was eventually raised to help the starving nations.

Many countries in the world still have similar problems today. What can we do to help?

We Are the World

Words and Music by Michael Jackson and Lionel Richie

1. There comes a time when we heed a cer-tain call, __ when the

world must come to-geth-er as one. There are peo-ple dy - ing __ and it's

time to __ lend a hand __ to life, the great-est gift __ of all. __

2. We can't go on _____ pre - tend-ing day __ by day, ___
3. Send them your heart _____ so they'll know that some - one cares __

that some-one, some-where, will soon make a change. We are
and their lives will be ___ strong-er and free. As

all a part _ of ___ God's great big fam - i - ly __ and the
God has shown _ us ___ by turn-ing stone _ to bread, _ so we

truth, you know, love is all ___ we ___ need.
all must lend a help - ing ___ hand.

We are the world, __ we are the chil - dren. We are the ones __

__ to make a bright-er day, __ so let's __ start giv - ing. There's a

choice we're mak - ing, ___ we're sav-ing our __ own lives. __ It's true, __

1.

__ we make a bet - ter day, __ just you __ and me. ___

2. **3.** *Fine*

(repeat Refrain ad lib)

___ When you're ___ down and out, _ there seems no hope _ at all; _

but if you just be - lieve, _ there's no way ___ we can fall. _

__ Let us re - al-ize _ that a change will on - ly come _ when

D.S. al Fine

we stand to-geth-er as one.

Part of our responsibility in today's world is to get to know our neighbors from other countries. How many musical styles from different cultures can you recognize in this song?

Take Me to the World .... Jon Ehrlich

Rhythm—
The Heartbeat of Music

When you find yourself clapping your hands or tapping your feet to a piece of music, you are responding to rhythm. It is the foundation upon which music is built. Every culture has its own unique way of creating and using rhythm in its music.

As you sing "Put On a Happy Face," tap your hands on your knees or on your desk each time you see an X above the music. This represents the **beat** of the music.

Put On a Happy Face

Words by Lee Adams   Music by Charles Strouse

Gray skies are gon-na   clear up, ___   put on   a hap-py   face;

Brush off the clouds and cheer up, ___   put on   a hap-py   face.

Take off the gloom-y   mask of trag - e-dy,   it's not your style;

You'll look so good that you'll be glad _ ya' de - cid-ed to smile! _

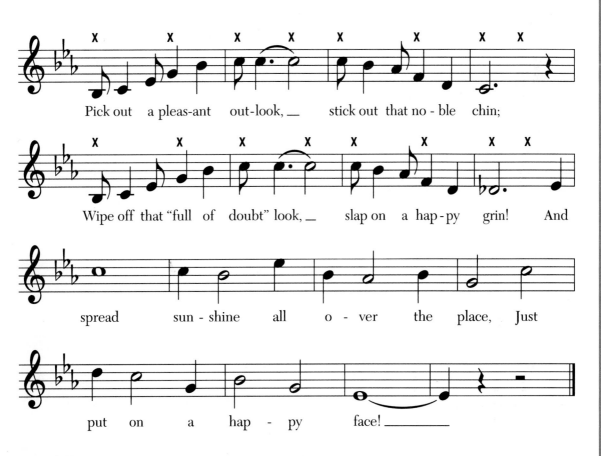

Pick out a pleas-ant out-look, __ stick out that no - ble chin;

Wipe off that "full of doubt" look, __ slap on a hap-py grin! And

spread sun - shine all o - ver the place, Just

put on a hap - py face! _____

Begin with a steady beat. Tap a steady quarter-note rhythm.

Accent every other note by chanting the word *pass* while tapping.

pass   pass

The beats are grouped in twos—a **meter** in 2. Bar lines are usually placed between each grouping.

Meter signatures tell musicians what the meter grouping is and what note is going to represent the beat. The bottom number of the signature tells what kind of note represents the beat; so $\frac{2}{4}$ means that a quarter note represents the beat and $\frac{2}{2}$ means that a half note represents the beat. The main idea, however, is that if the top number of the meter signature is 2, the meter is in 2 no matter what note represents the beat.

"Put on a Happy Face" on page 8 is in a meter of 2. Its meter signature is $\frac{2}{2}$, which means the beats are grouped in twos and a half note represents the beat.

Let's return to a meter signature of $\frac{2}{4}$. Continue to keep a steady beat, but divide the beat in half by chanting the word *basket*.

bas - ket   bas - ket   bas - ket   bas - ket

We can also divide the beat in half again. Tap the beat, but this time say the word *interference* each time you tap.

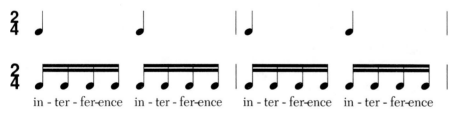

in - ter - fer-ence   in - ter - fer-ence   in - ter - fer-ence   in - ter - fer-ence

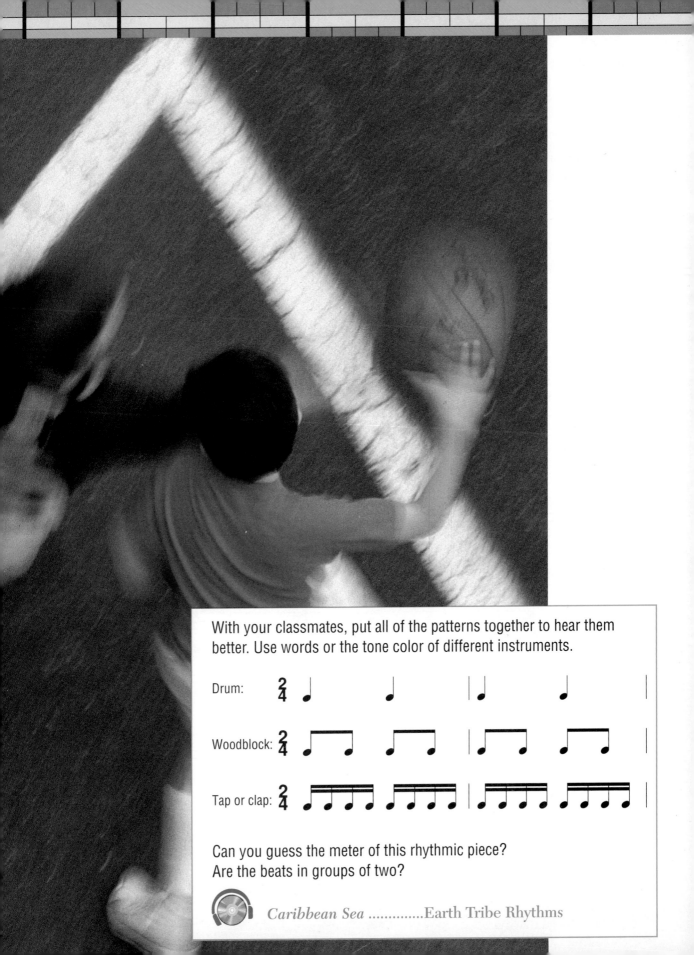

With your classmates, put all of the patterns together to hear them better. Use words or the tone color of different instruments.

Drum:

Woodblock:

Tap or clap:

Can you guess the meter of this rhythmic piece?
Are the beats in groups of two?

Caribbean Sea ....Earth Tribe Rhythms

Meter in 4

In this song from the West Indies, notice how the rhythm of the words controls the rhythm of the melody and accompaniment.

Jamaica Farewell

Words and Music by Irving Burgie

1. Down the way where the nights are gay ___ and the
2. Sounds of laugh - ter are ev - 'ry - where ___ and the

sun shines dai - ly on the moun - tain - top, ___
danc - ing girls ___ are sway - ing to and fro. ___

I took a trip on a sail - ing ship ___ and when I
I must de - clare that my heart is there ___ tho' I have

reached Ja - mai - ca I made a stop, ___ But I'm
been from Maine ___ to old Mex - i - co, ___ But I'm

To add harmony to the song, play the autoharp in this rhythm pattern.

This countermelody for bells, recorder, or keyboard goes with the refrain.

REFRAIN

Sad to say I'm on my way, ___ won't be back for man-y a day. ___ My heart is down, _ my head is turn-ing a-round, _ I had to leave a lit-tle girl in King-ston town. ___

Listen to this famous version of "Jamaica Farewell" performed by Harry Belafonte.

Jamaica Farewell ....Irving Burgie

Meter in 3

Listen to this recording of a waltz. Can you feel that the beats are grouped in threes?

Masquerade Suite, "Waltz" (excerpt)
.................Aram Khachaturian

Look at the way these quarter notes are grouped in threes.

Place bar lines in the right places and add the appropriate meter signature, and you have a meter in 3!

How are the beats grouped in "My White Horse"?

My White Horse *(Mi caballo blanco)*

English Words by Alice Firgau   *Words and Music by Francisco Flores del Campo*

Guitar: capo 2

1. My horse is like the sun - rise, _ As white as ear - ly dawn.
   Es mi ca - ba - llo blan - co, _ Co - mo un a - ma - ne - cer,
2. On wings of joy I rode him, _ My fast and faith - ful steed;
   En a - las de u-na di - cha _ Mi ca - ba - llo co - rrió.

We al - ways roam to - geth - er, _ He's my good and loy - al friend.
Siem-pre jun - ti - tos va - mos, _ Es mi a - mi - go más _ fiel.
On wings of woe he took me, _ Gal - lop - ing at great _ speed.
En a - las de u-na pe - na _ El tam-bién me lle - vó.

How he gal - lops, how he gal - lops, How swift - ly _ he goes. _
Mi ca - ba - llo, mi ca - ba - llo, Ga - lo - pan - do va, _

How he gal - lops, how he gal - lops, A - way _ he goes.
Mi ca - ba - llo, mi ca - ba - llo, Se va y _ se va.

Ah _____ Hmm. _____

3. I ask my heav'nly Father,
   and this He does know,
   When to His side He calls me,
   on my faithful horse I'll go.

3. *Al Taita Dios le pido*
   Y él lo sabe muy bien,
   Que a su lado me llama
   En mi caballo iré.

Rock Steady Reggae

It was in Jamaica in the late 1950s that a new style of music and dance emerged. It was called *ska,* or blue beat. The name was used to describe songs that had a strong emphasis on the offbeat and that were usually fairly fast and bright. This early recording by Bob Marley and the Wailers is a good example of ska style.

One Love (excerpt)
.............Bob Marley
and the Wailers

The next Jamaican musical fashion slowed down the tempo a bit and emphasized the bass line. The new songs were termed *rock steady.* In 1966 a rock steady song called "Do the Reggay" appeared and somehow the term **reggae** stuck. The style soon became associated with Rastafarianism (based on the worship of Haile Selassie I, former emperor of Ethiopia) and social discontent. Bob Marley was the most famous musician to represent these beliefs in reggae music.

Modern reggae has been influenced by African American music, rock, and traditional African Jamaican music (which is actually a blend of western African and British elements). All of these styles come together in reggae to produce a sound that has provided a sense of identity and belonging to all Jamaicans.

Bob Marley

Reggae Rhythm Complex

Follow this procedure to build up a reggae sound from a solid foundation. First, set up a rock steady beat of about one beat per second, in sets of four. Now, clap on the offbeats (2 and 4), as indicated in the chart.

1	2	3	4	1	2	3	4
	2		4		2		4

Next, add some harmony. Choose two triads that are next to each other. A-C-E and G-B-D work well. Dividing each beat in half, skip the first half, then play on the second. Repeat the routine set out in the chart as many times as you like.

	1	2	3	4	1	2	3	4
CLAP		2		4		2		4
HARMONY	E C A	E C A	E C A	E C A	D B G	D B G	D B G	D B G

A percussion line (using hi-hat cymbals, shaker, or drums) can be added by dividing the beat once more. Each beat, therefore, will have four percussion taps. (See the chart below.)

Finally, add a bass line. Use the low end of a keyboard, a large xylophone, or, best of all, a bass guitar. The bass, which takes its notes from the harmony, plays one note on each rock steady beat. The last chart shows how this part fits in with all the others.

	1	2	3	4	1	2	3	4
CLAP		2		4		2		4
HARMONY								
HI-HAT								
BASS	A	E	A	E	G	D	G	D

Reggae Today

Here is a modern reggae song made popular by Bob Marley's son, Ziggy. Try using a reggae rhythm complex to accompany the recording.

Give a Little Love

Words and Music by Al Hammond and Diane Warren

We got to give a lit-tle love, have _ a lit-tle hope, make _

_ this world a lit-tle bet - ter. Oh-oh whoah, Oh - oh whoah.

1. Liv-ing in this cra-zy world, _ so caught up in the con-fu - sion.
2. Got the wars _ on our minds, _ got the trou-bles on our shoul-ders.

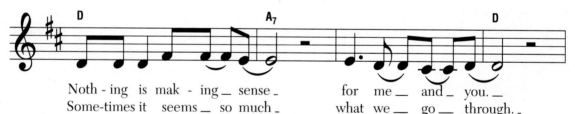

Noth - ing is mak - ing _ sense _ for me _ and _ you. _
Some-times it seems _ so much _ what we _ go _ through. _

May-be we can find a way, _ there's _ got to be a so-lu - tion,
May-be if we take the time, _ time _ to un-der-stand _ each oth - er,

How to make a bright-er day, _ What do _ we do? } We got to
We can learn to make it right. _ What do _ we do?

give a lit-tle love, have _ a lit-tle hope, make _ this world a lit-tle bet - ter.

Try a lit-tle more, hard - er than be-fore, let's do what we can do to-geth - er.

Oh _ whoah-oh, ____ We can ev-en make it bet - ter, yeah. _

1.
D   7   (last time
                       repeat refrain ad lib)

Oh whoah, _ la, la, la, On-ly if we try. ___ ___We got to

2. D   (Bm)   (Em)

_ If ev-'ry-bo-dy took some-bo-dy by the hand, _

(Em)   (Bm)   (Em)

___ ___ May-be ev-'ry-one _ could learn to love _ and

A₇   D   A₇

un-der-stand. _ Oh whoah, _ We can real-ly make it bet -

D   A₇
(2nd time to Refrain)

- ter, yeah. _ Oh whoah, _ la, la, la, On-ly if we try. _ (We got to)

Rhythm and Meter — Mixing Sixes

Take a look at these six eighth-notes. ♪ ♪ ♪ ♪ ♪ ♪

They can be divided in a number of ways using **accents**.

1. $\frac{6}{8}$ ♪ ♪ ♪ ♪ ♪ ♪   2. $\frac{6}{8}$ ♪ ♪ ♪ ♪ ♪ ♪

Here is an easier way to show the groups.

1. $\frac{6}{8}$ ♫ ♫ ♫   2. $\frac{6}{8}$ ♫♫ ♫♫

Sometimes music in a pattern of six alternates between accenting groups of two and groups of three.

Try this chant. The words fall naturally into rhythm patterns in groups of two ($\frac{6}{8}$) or in groups of three ($\frac{3}{4}$).

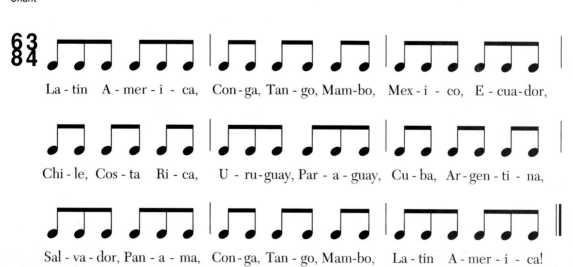

Latin America

Chant

$\frac{6}{8} \frac{3}{4}$

La - tin A - mer - i - ca, Con - ga, Tan - go, Mam - bo, Mex - i - co, E - cua - dor,

Chi - le, Cos - ta Ri - ca, U - ru - guay, Par - a - guay, Cu - ba, Ar - gen - ti - na,

Sal - va - dor, Pan - a - ma, Con - ga, Tan - go, Mam - bo, La - tin A - mer - i - ca!

In the musical play *West Side Story*, there is a song about Puerto Ricans living in New York City. The song has rhythms that are traditionally Latin American. It also uses alternating groups of three and two as in the chant.

GROUPS

OF

THREE

AND

TWO

 West Side Story, "America" ....Leonard Bernstein

Another Way to Mix Twos and Threes

A dance from *Carmina Burana* by Carl Orff also mixes twos and threes. However, this time they occur in irregular patterns. The music begins this way.

Try clapping the rhythm pattern, then listen to the way it happens in the music.

 Carmina Burana, "Tanz"...................Carl Orff

How are groups of two and three used in this piece?

 A Ceremony of Carols, "Balulalow" ....Benjamin Britten

Combining Meters

You have learned that the meter of a piece determines how the beats are grouped and what note represents the beat. In "Latin America," you saw how groups of six notes can be grouped differently to create alternating meters of ¾ and 6/8.

What do you think would happen if many different meters were combined in one piece? Sound ridiculous? Famous composer P.D.Q. Bach (also known as Peter Schickele) did just that.

First he started the cellos and string basses with a meter signature of ¾.

Then the trumpets, violins, and violas enter in 6/8.

Next come the basses and altos of the chorus in 2/4.

Hap - py Birth-day! Hap - py Birth-day! Hap - py Birth-day!

The rest of the chorus (sopranos and tenors) enters in 3/2.

Hap - py Birth - day! Hap - py Birth - day!

Finally, the vocal soloists are introduced—in 4/4! Here is part of their melody.

Any of these entrances by instruments or the choir would be fine by itself. But after introducing one group, the composer continued to add groups until all of them were playing in different meter signatures at the same time! How do you think this will sound?

Birthday Ode to "Big Daddy" Bach ..............P.D.Q. Bach (Peter Schickele)

Sound and Pitch

Strike a piano key, pluck a guitar string, or blow into a clarinet. You have made a sound. In fact, you have made a tone with definite **pitch**.

Now strike a drum, hit a woodblock, or tap two finger cymbals together. You have made a sound, but it has no definite pitch.

Both kinds of sound—pitched and unpitched—can be used to make music.

Play the familiar melody below using any pitched instrument and any set of unpitched percussion instruments. You can even invent your own percussion set from objects in your classroom.

Bonnie Raitt

Phil Collins

Pitched   Unpitched

In this song, all the pitches are next to each other. The melody moves by step upward and downward.

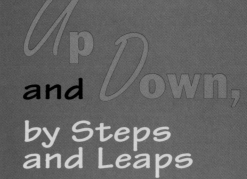

Annie Lee

Words and Music by Mary Hoffman

There is a val - ley, a far a - way val - ley. 'Twas

there that I first saw my sweet ___ An - nie Lee. Though the

years have gone by, and my home's in the moun - tains, I'll

nev - er for - get her, my sweet An - nie Lee.

Here is a countermelody that can be sung or played on bells, recorder, or keyboard. Notice that the pitches do not move stepwise. The notes leap from pitch to pitch.

An - nie, An - nie, An - nie, my An - nie Lee.

I'll nev - er, nev - er for - get her, my An - nie Lee.

The Tonal Center

Cadence and Phrase

Here's a melody—a **phrase**—without a final note. Even without knowing what it is, you will probably be able to sing the last note correctly.

The rest of the phrase seems to lead you to the last note. This kind of phrase ending is called a **cadence**. A cadence is like a rest stop. The melody will seem to lead to that point and rest comfortably there.

Often the final note of a piece will be at the **tonal center**. The note at the tonal center is the key note. Every scale is named for the key note.

As you sing this song from Bolivia, decide what the difference is between the two measures in color.

The Butterfly *(La mariposa)*

English Words by Aura Kontra   *Folk Song from Bolivia*

Guitar: capo 2

La la la la lai   la   lai   la lai   la   lai   lai   lai   lai   lai,

La la la la lai   la   lai   la lai   la   lai   la la la la la   lai   lai   lai.

Hear the rat-tles' rhyth-mic beat,   Call-ing   us   to   sing and dance
Al   son de   las   ma-tra-cas   to-dos can-tan   y   bai-lan

to   the live-ly   sound.   Clap   your hands now,   *(clap)*
La   mo-re-na-da.   Con   las   pal-mas,

kick   your heels up,   *(stamp)*   turn   your part-ner 'round.
con   los   ta-cos.   ¡Vi-va   la   fies-ta!

Turn   your part-ner 'round,   turn   your part-ner 'round.   *(clap)*
¡Vi-va   la   fies-ta!   ¡Vi-va   la   fies-ta!

Building *Melody*

Contour

Making a melody means deciding what shape it will take, or what the **contour** of the tune will be. It could be very jagged, like a city skyline.

Symphony No. 1 in D, "Gavotte" (excerpt) .... Sergei Prokofiev

Or it could move stepwise and be as smooth as rolling hills.

Jesu, Joy of Man's Desiring ....J. S. Bach

In vocal music, **imagery** helps determine the melodic line. For example, if you are singing about a mountaintop, you are probably going to ascend in your melody, as in the song "Jamaica Farewell."

moun - tain - top

The words *made a stop* actually come to a harmonic stop by ending the phrase on the tonal center, or key note.

made   a   stop

A composer can also choose to emphasize lyrics through a melody. Look at the phrase *We are all a part* from the song "We Are the World." The word *all* comes across strongly because it falls on the first and strongest beat. It is also the highest note, giving it even more importance.

We   are   all   a   part

Notice the emphasis the word *love* gets because of the approach to it by a leap.

you know, love is all __ we __ need

Here are some melodic contours drawn from melodies of songs you have learned. Can you discover which songs they represent?

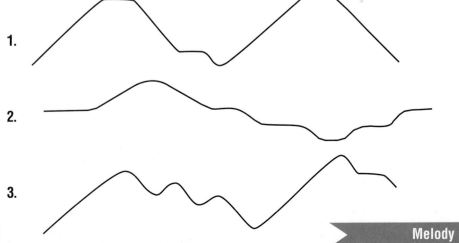

1.

2.

3.

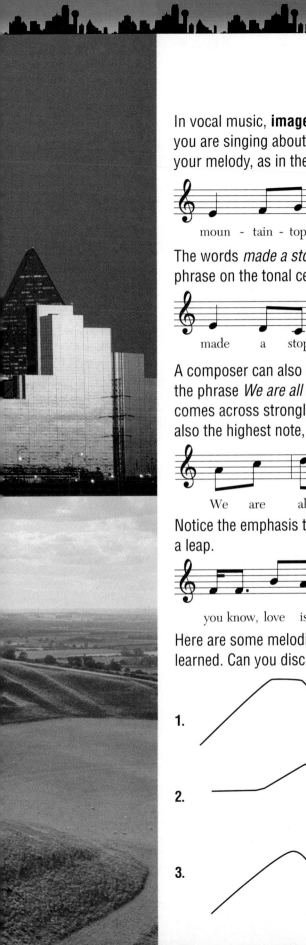

Extending a Melody

Here is a simple three-note melody.

You can extend it by repeating it,

or by inventing a new, contrasting melody.

So, two ways of extending a melody are **repetition** and **contrast**.

You can also repeat the original melody on new pitches. This repeating of a pattern on a different pitch is called a **sequence**.

How has the melody of "Tea for Two" been extended?

Tea for Two

Words by Irving Caesar   *Music by Vincent Youmans*

In "Tea for Two" the repeated three-note melody themes are contrasted at the cadences and at the end of the song.

Here is a famous country song that is also built using repeated patterns and contrast. The middle section contrasts with the rest of the song.

More Repetition and Contrast

On the Road Again

Words and Music by Willie Nelson   Arranged by Larry Eisman

On the   road a-gain. _____   Just can't wait to get   on the
          road a-gain. _____   Go-in'   pla-ces   that I've
          road a-gain. _____   Just can't wait to get   on the

road a-gain. _____   The life I love   is   mak-ing mu-sic with my
nev-er been. _____   ,   See-in' things that   I   may nev-er see a-
road a-gain. _____   The life I love   is   mak-ing mu-sic with my

friends, and   I can't wait to get   on the road _ a - gain. _____ On the
gain,   and   I can't wait to get   on the road _ a - gain. _____   ___
friends, and   I can't wait to get   on the road _ a - gain. _____ *Repeat entire song,
                                                              then go to Coda*

On the road a-gain, _____ Like a band of gyp-sies we go down the

high-way. _____ We're the best of friends, _ In - sist - ing that the

world keep turn-ing our way, _____ and our way, _____ Is on the

I can't wait to get on the road a - gain. _ And on the road a - gain. _

Listen to how the composer of this song performs it.

On the Road Again ....Willie Nelson

Harmony

When you sing or play more than one tone at a time, you create **harmony**.

Here is one way to create harmony. Start by singing this simple melody.

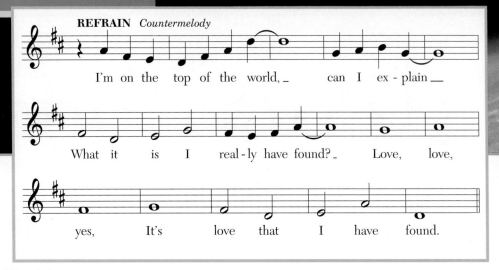

REFRAIN *Countermelody*

I'm on the top of the world, __ can I ex - plain __

What it is I real - ly have found? __ Love, love,

yes, It's love that I have found.

Top of the World

Words by John Bettis   Music by Richard Carpenter

1. Such a feel - in's com - in' o - ver me, _____ There is
2. Ev - 'ry - thing __ I want the world to be, _____ Is now

won - der in __ most ev - 'ry - thing __ I see; _____ Not a
com - ing true __ es - pe - cial - ly __ for me; _____ And the

cloud in the sky, __ got the sun in my eyes, and I
rea - son is clear, __ it's be - cause you are here, you're the

Now sing this song in **unison**—that is,
with everyone on the same pitches at the same time.

If you combine the melody at the top of page 34 with the
refrain of "Top of the World," the result is harmony!

A Musical Partnership

Here are two short and simple songs to learn.

Down the Ohio

River Shanty

The riv-er is up and the chan-nel is deep, The wind is stead-y and strong.

Oh, won't we have a jol-ly good time As we go sail-ing a - long.

REFRAIN

Melody

Down the riv-er, Oh, down the riv-er, Oh, down the riv-er we go - o - o.

Down the riv-er, Oh, down the riv-er, Oh, down the O - hi - o! _____

Vive L'Amour

Traditional College Song

1. Let ev'ry good fel-low now join in a song, *Vi-ve la com-pa - gnie!* __
2. Come all you good fel-lows and join in with me, *Vi-ve la com-pa - gnie!* __

Suc-cess to each oth-er and pass it a-long, *Vi-ve la com-pa - gnie!* __
And raise up your voic-es in close har-mo-ny, *Vi-ve la com-pa - gnie!* __

REFRAIN

Vi-ve la, vi-ve la, vi-ve l'a-mour, Vi-ve la, vi-ve la, vi-ve l'a-mour,

Vi - ve l'a-mour, Vi - ve l'a-mour, Vi - ve la com - pa - gnie! ___

Now be daring. Try performing the refrains of these two songs together. You are singing in harmony!

You have already learned how to create harmony by using a countermelody. Here is another way.

A *Canon*

The song "Catch a Falling Star" is a **canon**. In a canon, one voice begins the song followed by other voices, each entering at a later time, but singing the same song.

Catch a Falling Star

Words and Music by Paul Vance and Lee Pockriss

Catch a fall-ing star and put it in your pock-et, Nev-er let it fade a-
Catch a fall-ing star and put it in your pock-et, Save it for a rain-y

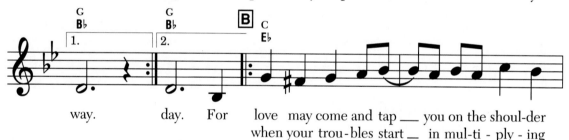

way.   day.   For love may come and tap __ you on the shoul-der
when your trou-bles start __ in mul-ti-ply-ing

some star-less night.   And just in case you think _ you want to hold her,
and they just might.   It's eas-y to for-get __ them with-out try-ing,

you'll have a pock-et full of star-light.
with just a pock-et full of star-light.   } Catch a fall-ing star and

Canons can be used in instrumental music, too. Listen to this movement from a symphony. Do you recognize the famous tune that is used? Can you hear where the imitation begins?

 Symphony No. 1 in D Major, Mvt. 3..........Gustav Mahler

A Round and a Round

A **round** is a kind of canon. When you come to the end of a round, simply go back to the beginning and start over.

Try this three-part round from Israel.

Mallet instruments, Keyboard, or Recorder

Yibane Amenu

Round from Israel

In our land we shall re - build our na - tion.
Yi - ba - ne a - me - nu b' - ar - tse - nu;

Build our na - tion in our land; In our land,
B' - ar - tse - nu yi - ba - ne; Yi - ba - ne,

in our land, in our land, in our land.
yi - ba - ne, yi - ba - ne, yi - ba - ne.

Now you're ready for a five-part round.

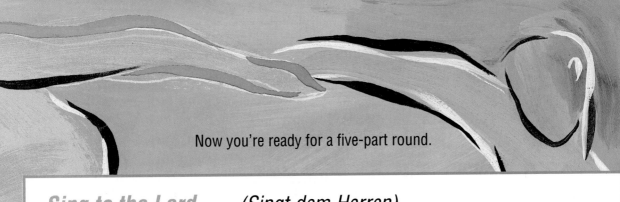

Sing to the Lord   (Singt dem Herren)

English Words by Don Kalbach   Five-part Round by Michael Praetorius

Sing to the Lord, — Sing to Him with ju - bi - la - tion,
Singt dem — Herr - en, sin - get ihm und ju - bi - lie - ret

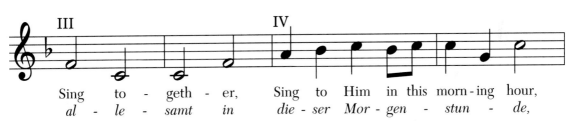

Sing to - geth - er, Sing to Him in this morn - ing hour,
al - le - samt in die - ser Mor - gen - stun - de,

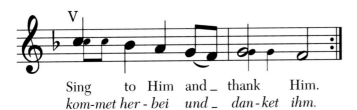

Sing to Him and — thank Him.
kom-met her - bei und — dan - ket ihm.

Vocal Tone Color

A human voice can make many different kinds of sounds—it can sing, talk, shout, or whisper. Each sound is different from the others. In fact, your voice is made up of a combination of unique qualities. No one else has a voice with the same **tone color** as yours.

One characteristic of the human voice is **range**—how high or low it sounds. As you listen to the recording of this spiritual, notice the different ranges of the singers.

Little Wheel A-Turnin'

African American Spiritual

1. There's a lit-tle wheel a-turn-in' in my heart, There's a
2. There's a lit-tle song a-sing-in' in my heart, There's a
3. There's a lit-tle love a-liv-in' in my heart, There's a

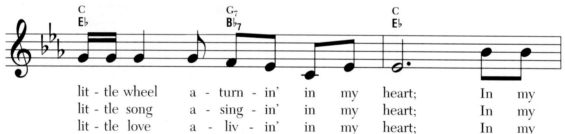

lit-tle wheel a-turn-in' in my heart; In my
lit-tle song a-sing-in' in my heart; In my
lit-tle love a-liv-in' in my heart; In my

heart, _____ in my heart. _____ There's a
heart, _____ in my heart. _____ There's a
heart, _____ in my heart. _____ There's a

lit-tle wheel a-turn-in' in my heart.
lit-tle song a-sing-in' in my heart.
lit-tle love a-liv-in' in my heart.

4. There's a little bell a-ringin' . . .

5. There's a little drum a-beatin' . . .

Name that Mood!

What do you think the **mood** of this song should be? How will the mood affect your performance? After you have listened to the recording, plan a different performance of "Music Goes with Anything." How will you change the tone color of your voice?

Music Goes with Anything

Words and Music by Sarah and Robert Sterling

Mu - sic keeps me snap-pin' my fin - gers. Mu - sic keeps me

tap-pin' my toes. _ Mu - sic goes with an - y - thing, _ and with

mu - sic, an - y-thing goes!   mu - sic, an - y-thing goes!

VERSE

1. What wakes me up in the morn - in'? What bright-ens up my

drear-y day? __ What grabs my heart with-out a warn-in' and

takes it up, up, and a-way? __ Bar-ber-shop, jazz, rock, op-'ra, and dis - co,

all have a charm that en - thralls. __ They left my heart in

to Refrain

San Fran-cis - co, in Pa-ris, and in Mon-te-zu-ma's halls! Don'-cha know that

2. Rag - time! Two good beats an' I'm danc - in', Sou - sa has me

march-in' right a-long! Gil-bert and Sul - li - van are en - tranc - in',

Choosing a *Medium*

The Artist's Medium

When an artist chooses a subject to express visually, he or she must choose the **medium** in which to work.

An artist may choose oil paint, for example, as the best medium for a particular work of art. Another artist may decide to interpret that same subject through sculpture. Here is one subject—a bowl of apples—that has been expressed in five different media.

The Composer's Medium

A composer must choose a *musical* medium to express an idea. This is only one of the many decisions a composer must make, but it is a very important one.

In music, the medium consists of the instruments, voices, or combinations of the two that will be used to create the desired sound.

Listen to this piece by the French composer Maurice Ravel. The composer made two different choices: he wrote it first for piano, then for orchestra.

Le Tombeau de Couperin, "Minuet" (piano excerpt) ....Ravel

Le Tombeau de Couperin, "Minuet" (orchestra excerpt) ....Ravel

*M*eet the *C*omposer

Maurice Ravel led a distinguished musical career in France as both a composer and pianist. He wrote many famous piano pieces, but is best known for his orchestral piece *Bolero*. Ravel would often write a piece for piano and then rewrite the same piece for orchestra, as he did with the "Minuet."

Ravel was considered to be one of the most skillful orchestrators of his time. His pieces are full of beautiful orchestral "color." His style has often been copied by composers of television and movie music.

Ravel greatly admired American composer George Gershwin — he even used a jazz style for one of his piano concertos!

Maurice Ravel (1875–1937)

Choosing a Palette

The Artist's Palette

An artist's palette holds a variety of colors. The artist chooses the colors that will help express an idea or feeling about the subject of a painting.

Vibrant, warm reds and oranges? Cool, liquid blues and greens? Shimmering yellows and golds?

Matisse, Henri. *Les Poissons Rouge*, 1912. Pushkin Museum, Moscow.
©1995 Succession H. Matisse/ARS, New York. Photo: Scala/Art Resource.

Les Poissons Rouge   *Henri Matisse*

The colors in a painting may be quiet and subdued or bright and bold. It all depends on the choices the artist makes to express his or her ideas visually.

The Composer's Palette

The composer's palette is as varied and colorful as the painter's. Composers choose instruments with specific sound qualities to express ideas musically.

Listen to these two short musical sketches. Think of them as musical pictures or as abstract, colorful designs. One is dark and somber and one is bright and cheerful.

Pictures at an Exhibition, "Bydlo" (excerpt) ....Modest Mussorgsky

Candide, "Overture" (excerpt) ....Leonard Bernstein

A painter can use contrasting colors or may highlight sections of a painting to make the work more interesting.

A composer can do the same thing with music by combining tone colors of different instruments.

Piccolo

Flute

Oboe

English horn

Clarinet

Bassoon

Horn

Trumpet

Trombone

Tuba

Timpani

Percussion

I

Violins

II

Viola

Cello

Bass

The Colors of the Orchestra

Painting with Sound

As we have said, a composer paints pictures and designs with musical sound. The particular sound an instrument makes is called **tone color**. Tone color is affected by the materials used to make the instrument as well as by the size and shape of the instrument.

Tone color is linked to the method of sound production, whether a sound is made by scraping, blowing, striking, or in some other way.

Listen to the opening of this orchestral piece by Berlioz and notice the colorful use of the instruments.

 Roman Carnival Overture (excerpt) ....Hector Berlioz

Meet the Composer

Hector Berlioz became a famous composer in France when he was still quite young. He had a very colorful personality and often did things that shocked a lot of people. He was a little like some of our rock stars!

He wrote many famous works, including *Symphonie fantastique,* which even today is one of the most popular symphony pieces.

Berlioz was very good at choosing and using the colors of the orchestra. He is often spoken of as a musical "colorist." Many of the special effects he created were far ahead of his time.

Hector Berlioz (1803-1869)

Woodwinds

A symphony orchestra contains the instrumental colors a composer needs to paint musical pictures. The conductor of the orchestra knows which instruments are to be playing by looking at a score. Refer to the orchestral score on page 50 as you read about the families of instruments.

The woodwind instruments are first at the top of the score and are listed according to pitch.

The piccolo is very similar to the flute, but it is smaller and has a higher, more piercing sound.

Lieutenant Kijé Suite, Mvt. 1 (excerpt: piccolo) ....Prokofiev

The flute has a high, sweet sound. It is perfect for long, flowing melodies.

Daphnis and Chloé Suite No. 2
(excerpt: flute).................Ravel

Next in order on the score are the oboe and the English horn. The oboe has an exotic, nasal sound.

Polovtsian Dance No. 2
(excerpt: oboe)
..................Borodin

Clarinet

Oboe

The English horn sounds similar to the oboe, but darker and deeper.

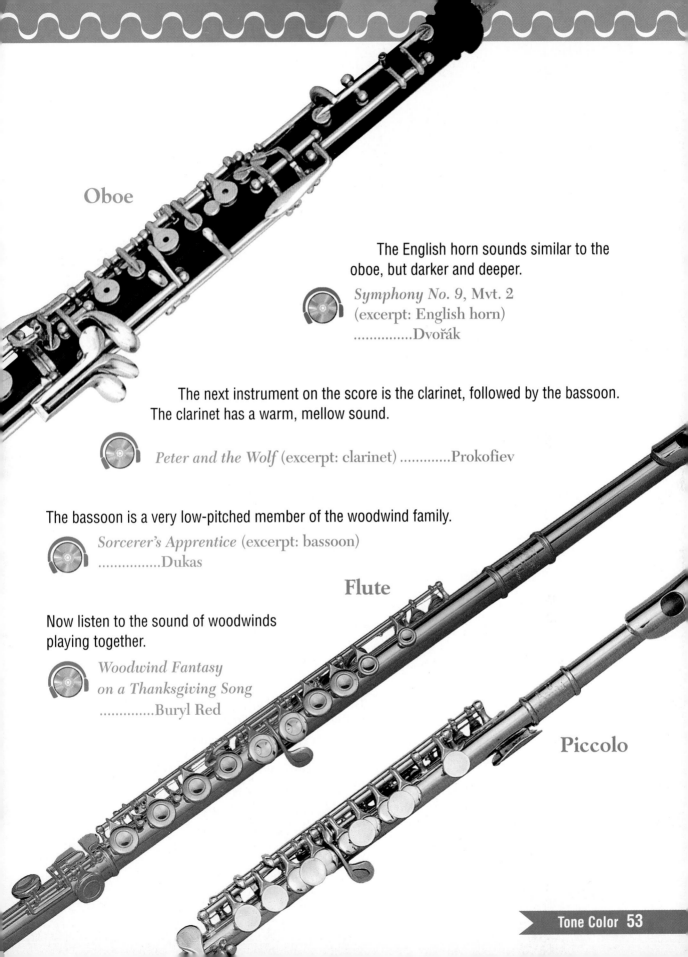 *Symphony No. 9, Mvt. 2* (excerpt: English horn) ....Dvořák

The next instrument on the score is the clarinet, followed by the bassoon. The clarinet has a warm, mellow sound.

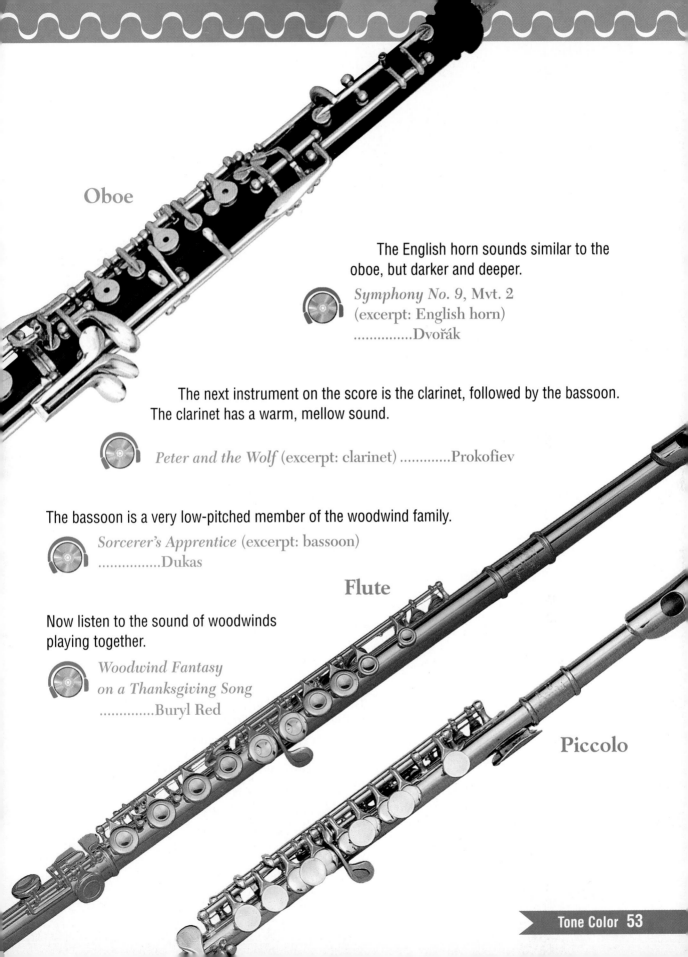 *Peter and the Wolf* (excerpt: clarinet) ....Prokofiev

The bassoon is a very low-pitched member of the woodwind family.

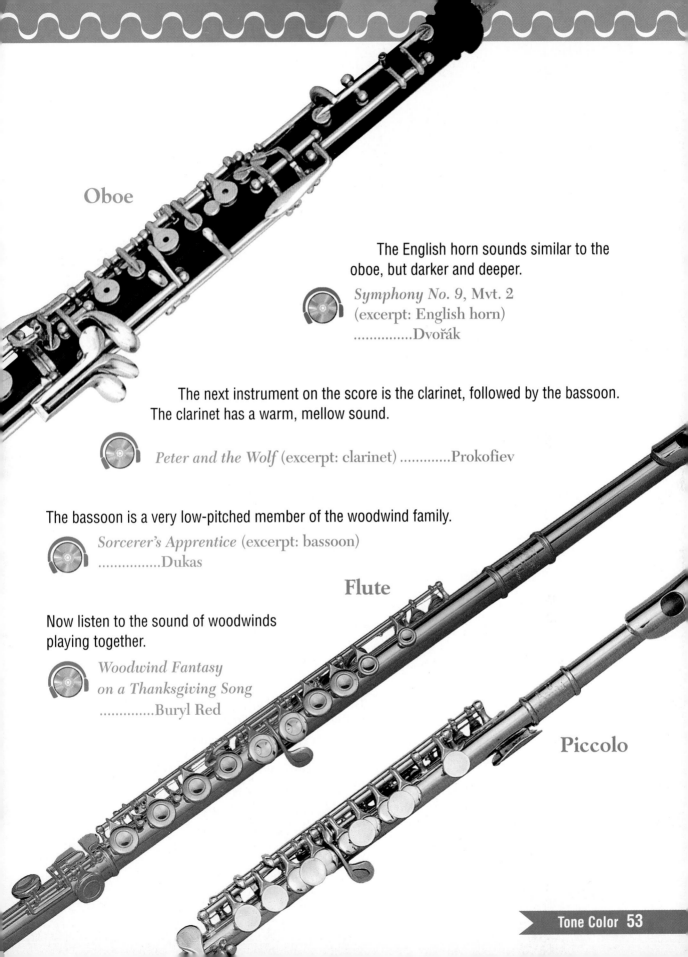 *Sorcerer's Apprentice* (excerpt: bassoon) ....Dukas

Flute

Now listen to the sound of woodwinds playing together.

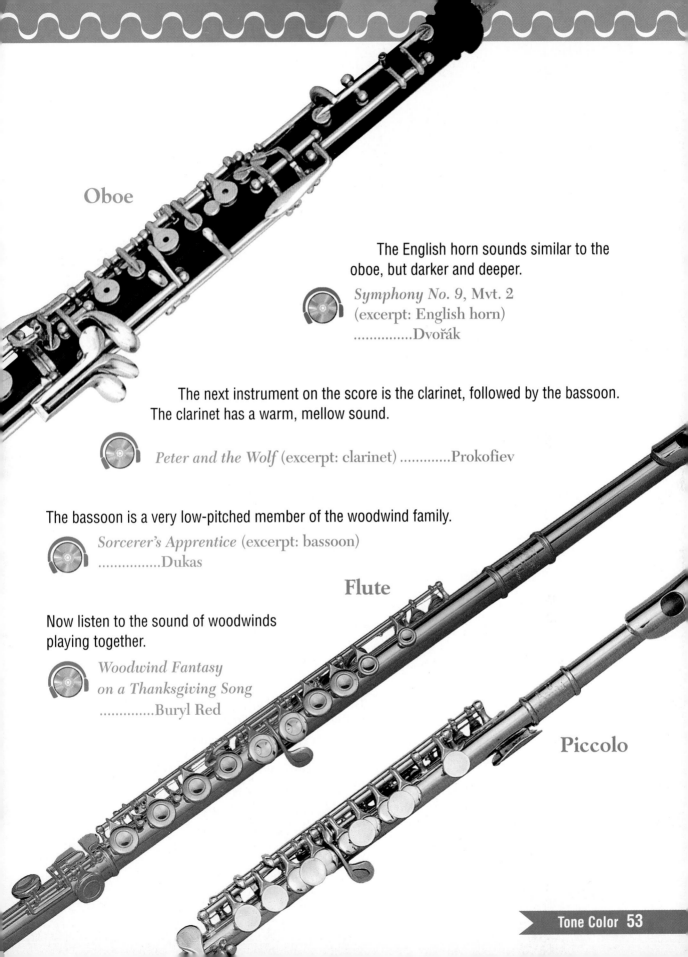 *Woodwind Fantasy on a Thanksgiving Song* ....Buryl Red

Piccolo

Brass

The family of brass instruments comes next. The most noticeable characteristic of modern brass instruments is their coiled tubing. Without it, they would take up too much space to play. An ancient kind of trumpet with straight tubing is still sometimes used today for special occasions. Such trumpets are typically used to make announcements or to introduce very important people.

The French horn appears first in the brass section of the score. Its mellow sound goes especially well with woodwind instruments.

Till Eulenspiegel's Merry Pranks (excerpt: French horn) ....Strauss

The trumpet can play a number of sounds and styles. It is very effective in fanfares and marches. Listen to this familiar march from a famous opera.

Aida, "Grand March"
(excerpt: trumpet).............Verdi

The trombone is the only instrument that changes pitch with the use of a slide.

Tannhäuser, "Pilgrims' Chorus"
(excerpt: trombone) ....Wagner

The tuba is the lowest in pitch of all the brass instruments.

Pictures at an Exhibition, "Bydlo"
(excerpt: tuba).............Mussorgsky

Brass instruments have loud, assertive voices. However, they can also play softly and sound very lyrical when the music calls for it. Listen for both styles in this arrangement for brass choir.

Echo Song.............Orlando di Lasso

Trombone

Percussion

The percussion section adds excitement and color to the sound of the orchestra. Percussion instruments are most often used to emphasize the rhythm of a piece of music.

Symphony No. 9, "March"
(excerpt: percussion)...........Beethoven

Percussion instruments are generally divided into two groups: those that play definite pitches and those that play sounds with no definite pitch.

The snare drum and bass drum are instruments of indefinite pitch. They usually play strong rhythm patterns. The cymbals add splashes of sound.

Battery (excerpt: snare drum, bass drum, cymbals) ....Linda Williams

Percussion instruments of definite pitch are called *mallet instruments*. The xylophone, orchestra bells, marimba, and chimes are all mallet instruments and can be used to play melodies.

Listen to the sound of the xylophone. The composer wanted to use an instrument that could sound like old bones!

Carnival of the Animals, "Fossils"
(excerpt: xylophone)...........Saint-Saëns

Snare drum

The chimes are often used to represent church bells or clocks.

Pictures at an Exhibition, "Great Gate of Kiev"
(excerpt: chimes) ....Mussorgsky

The orchestra bells, marimba, and other mallet instruments are often used to reinforce a melody line played by another instrument. Although they can be used to play tunes, they are often used to create interesting colors or textures.

The timpani, sometimes called kettledrums, can also play definite pitches. Listen for the timpani in this excerpt.

Symphony No. 9, "Scherzo"
(excerpt: timpani) ....Beethoven

Now listen to this piece written only for percussion instruments.

Intrusion of the Hunter
...............Laurie MacGregor

Timpani

Strings

The orchestral string instruments are the violin, viola, cello, and string bass. The string section forms the main body of any Western symphony orchestra.

The violin is the highest sounding orchestral string instrument, followed by the viola, cello, and string bass. There are some notes that are the same on the violin, viola, and cello.

Violins have a wide range and can play in very high registers.

Young Person's Guide to the Orchestra
(excerpt: violin) ....Britten

The viola is a larger version of the violin. Its sound is dark and mellow.

Piano Concerto No. 2, Mvt. 3
(excerpt: viola)
...............Rachmaninoff

String bass

The low-voiced cello has a rich, mellow sound.

 *Symphony No. 5*, Mvt. 2
(excerpt: cello) ....Tchaikovsky

The string bass has a very deep voice.

Lieutenant Kijé Suite, "Romance"
(excerpt: string bass) ....Prokofiev

Listen to the way string instruments sound when playing together on the same pitches.

The Planets,
"Jupiter".........Holst

Violin

Cello

Form
A Musical Blueprint

What is the first thing you do before putting together a model? Of course—read the directions. You can imagine what it might look like if you tried building it without them!

When an architect is designing a house, he or she creates a blueprint so that the builder will know exactly where to put each section.

Composers, like architects, have plans for their compositions. Musical ideas and events cannot be put together in just any way. Try singing this version of a familiar song.

See how they run! Three blind mice. They all ran af-ter the

farm-er's wife, See how they run! They all ran af-ter the farm-er's wife,

Music Taking Shape

The use of **contrast** is extremely important to a composer when "building" music. If a piece of music were the same from beginning to end, we would soon grow tired of it. "Jamaica Farewell" on page 12 has two main contrasting sections. Therefore, we call its form AB.

Sometimes rhythm is used to show contrast between sections. In writing "Laranjeiras," the composer made a musical blueprint from two rhythms. The first rhythm begins the piece. The second rhythm introduces a contrasting section. Does the first rhythm return at the end?

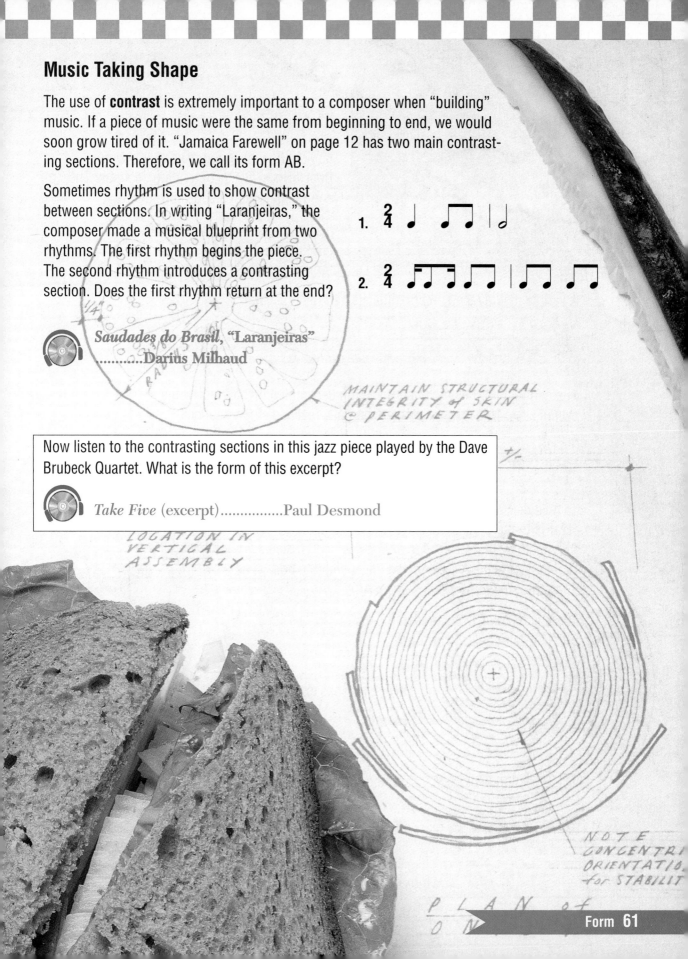

Saudades do Brasil, "Laranjeiras"
............Darius Milhaud

Now listen to the contrasting sections in this jazz piece played by the Dave Brubeck Quartet. What is the form of this excerpt?

Take Five (excerpt)...............Paul Desmond

Compare and Contrast

Look at how the composer of "No-Name Bossa Nova" uses contrasting sections. The song begins with a short introduction.

A simple melody then enters—the start of the A section.

The contrasting melody in the B section uses notes that are not in the original key. This is one clue that you have reached a new section.

To give the song a finished feeling, the composer returns to the original melody. This is indicated in the music by the words *D.S. al Coda*, which tell you to repeat only the A section and finish with the coda. Therefore, the form of the song is ABA.

Try playing an ABA accompaniment for "No-Name Bossa Nova" using percussion instruments.

Here's the A section, to be played on cabasas.

Shake

The B section is played by scraping the guiro.

Scrape

No-Name Bossa Nova

Words and Music by Mary E. Hoffman

Do the No-Name Bos-sa No-va, __ Do the No-Name Bos-sa No-va. __

We were _ danc-ing __ in the _ sha-dows _ While a __
danc-ing __ in the _ sha-dows _ But we __

qui-et _____ La-tin gui-tar strummed us _ a new tune, a
have-n't _____ thought of a name to give to _ that new tune, _ the

new tune _ that had no name.
new tune _ that has no name. } Do the No-Name Bos-sa No-va, __

Do the No-Name Bos-sa No-va. __ We _____ swayed to the rhy-thm __

_ De-signed _ for tro-pi-cal nights. __ This _____ me-lo-dy

haunts us, ___ It ech - oes with such de-lights _____ We're still __

Do the No-Name Bos-sa No - va. _____

What Form Is It?

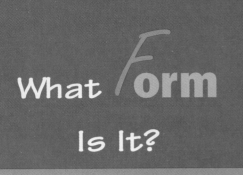

Sometimes a composer starts with a melody and then repeats it, but not exactly the same way. In form we call this a **variant**.

Can you find the variants in this song?

It's a Good Day

Words and Music by Peggy Lee and Dave Barbour

Forming a *Rondo*

What do you get if you take a piece of music in ABA form, add another contrasting section, and end with the A section? That's right—**rondo** form, otherwise known as ABACA. Because it always returns to a familiar idea, a rondo is a richly satisfying form. Listen to this famous rondo written for piano.

Call Chart

1.	2.	3.	4.	5.	
(A)	[B]	(A)	△C	(A)	*Für Elise* ....Ludwig van Beethoven

Now try creating and performing a rondo based on excerpts from the book *The Way to Start a Day* by Byrd Baylor. A song to greet the morning will become the A section. Other tributes to the day will become the contrasting sections. You should try to use instrumentation that is appropriate to the cultures that are mentioned.

Narrator 1: The way to start a day is this—go outside and face the east and greet the sun with some kind of blessing or chant or song that you made yourself and keep for early morning.

(A) *Compose a short song with a meter in 4, using C as the tonal center. Choose from the following notes to build your melody.*

Use what you have learned about repetition, contrast, and sequence to lengthen the melody. Then add words, using the idea of standing in the glow of a sunrise.

Narrator 2: People have always known that a new day needs to be honored. Didn't they chant at dawn in the sun temples of Peru?

[B] *Compose a short melody for recorder. Use a meter in 3 and a tonal center of G. Choose from the following notes to build your melody.*

Accompany your recorder piece with a rhythm pattern on drum. You might begin with the following example.

(A) *Repeat song*

Narrator 3: *And didn't they drum sunrise songs in the Congo?*

(C) *Compose a rhythm piece for cowbell, shaker, and drums. It should have a meter in 2, and could use the following rhythms.*

(A) *Repeat song*

Narrator 1: Some people say there is a new sun every day—that it begins its life at dawn and lives for one day only.

Narrator 2: They say you have to welcome it and make a good day for it.

Narrator 3: You have to make a good world for it to live its one-day life in.

Group: And the way to start, they say, is just by looking east at dawn.

Narrator 1: When they look east tomorrow, you can too.

Narrator 2: Your song will be an offering.

Group: And you'll be one more person in one more place at one more time in the world saying hello to the sun, letting it know you are there. That's the way to start a day.

Theme and Variations

Another kind of form is **theme and variations**.

Themes, or musical ideas, can be varied in a number of ways. Composers can be very clever in the way they write variations. Often a composer chooses a familiar tune for a set of variations.

The theme can be played slower or faster, or with changed rhythm patterns. The theme can be turned upside down, or can be decorated with extra notes to make it fancier.

Here is a famous set of variations written by Charles Ives. As you listen to the recording, you will recognize the theme. In fact, you will be able to hear the theme in each variation. However, the personality of the melody has been changed completely in each variation.

Variations on "America" (excerpt)...........Ives

Meet the Composer

Charles Ives (1874-1954)

American composer Charles Ives lived all his life in New England. He was a prosperous insurance company executive who wrote music in his spare time.

His music was very experimental for his time. It was not appreciated by the public until he was quite old and no longer composing. In 1947, when Ives was in his 70s and retired, he was awarded a Pulitzer Prize for his Third Symphony.

Some pieces of music, particularly songs, are timeless. They seem to speak to every age.

"Scarborough Fair" is an old English folk song with origins that go back many centuries. It has come down to us in several versions. This version is one of the most popular.

Scarborough Fair

Folk Song from England

1. Are you go - ing to Scar-bor-ough Fair?
2. Tell her to make me a cam - bric shirt, } Pars-ley, sage, rose-mar-y, and thyme;
3. Tell her to wash it in yon - der well,

Re - mem-ber me to one who lives there,
With - out a seam or nee - dle work, } She once was a true love of mine.
Where nev - er rain or wa - ter fell,

Folk songs like this one are part of our heritage.

However, musical styles change from age to age. A musician can recognize, through musical clues, the era in which a certain piece of music was written.

Musical Time Travel

Let's take our song "Scarborough Fair" through a time trip from the Middle Ages to the present day. We will hear it as it might have been played in each of the different time periods.

Scarborough Fair
—Variation 1: Medieval

Scarborough Fair
—Variation 2: Renaissance

Scarborough Fair
—Variation 3: Baroque

Scarborough Fair—Variation 4: Classic

Scarborough Fair
—Variation 5:
Romantic

Scarborough Fair
—Variation 6:
Impressionistic

Call Chart

Styles Montage

Listen for the musical clues that will tell you the historical period for each of these musical excerpts. You should be able to identify the period by the style of the music.

1. *Hodie Christus natus est* ....Anonymous

2. *Gigue* ....Byrd

3. *Suite No. 3 in D Major,* "Air" ....J. S. Bach

4. *Piano Sonata in C Major,* Mvt. 1 ....Mozart

5. *Piano Concerto No. 2,* Mvt. 3 ....Rachmaninoff

6. *Nocturnes,* "Festivals" ....Debussy

7. *Symphony for Chamber Orchestra,* Op. 21 ....Webern

Over the years, many composers have used songs from their own countries when composing larger works. Johannes Brahms was given this chance in 1880 when the University of Breslau wanted to honor him.

Music from Germany

Gaudeamus igitur

College Song from Germany

Gau-de - a - mus i - gi-tur, Ju - ve-nes dum su - mus;
Hail to youth and hail to love! Hail to life so won-der-ful!

Post ju - cun-dam ju-ven-tu - tem, Post mo-les - tam se - nec-tu - tem,
We will toss a - side all care, ___ And with all our com-rades share ___

Nos ha - be - bit ___ hu - mus, Nos ha - be - bit ___ hu - mus.
One long round of ___ mer - ri - ment, One long round of ___ mer - ri - ment.

What Comes There O'er the Hill?
(Was kommt dort von der Höh'?)

College Song from Germany

1. What comes there o'er the hill? What comes there o'er the hill? What comes there
   Was kommt dort von der Höh'? Was kommt dort von der Höh'? Was kommt dort
2. It is the post-man, sure, it is the post-man, sure, It is the
   Es ist ein Pos - till - ion, es ist ein Pos - till - ion, Es ist ein

In those days it was expected of a musician, and especially a composer, to write a piece for such an occasion. Brahms decided to write an overture using German college songs. Here are three of the songs he used.

ov - er yon - der hill, yes, sir, yon - der hill, What comes there o'er the hill?
von der leder-nen Höh'? ça, ça, leder-nen Höh', Was kommt dort von der Höh'?
post-man yon - der sure, yes, sir, yon - der sure, It is the post-man sure.
leder-nen Pos - till - ion, ça, ça, Pos - till - ion, Es ist ein Pos - till - ion.

3. What does the postman bring? . . .   3. *Was bringt der Postillion?* . . .

4. He brings a fox with him, . . .   4. *Er bringt 'nen Fuchsen mit,* . . .

The Stately House   *(Wir hatten gebauet)*

College Song from Germany

The house we have built is so state - ly and strong, A
Wir hat - ten ge - bau - et ein statt - li - ches Haus, Und

for - tress and a shel - ter from storm and _ strife and wrong. A
drin auf Gott ver - trau - et trotz Wet - ter, _ Sturm und Graus. Und

for - tress and a shel - ter from storm and _ strife and wrong.
drin auf Gott ver - trau - et trotz Wet - ter, _ Sturm und Graus.

Songs in a Larger Work

As you listen to the way Brahms worked with the three songs you have just learned, follow the call chart beginning on page 78. You will see how he changed the songs slightly to fit in with his idea of a festival overture for a big university celebration.

Academic Festival Overture
...............Johannes Brahms

Meet the Composer

Johannes Brahms is famous not only for his arrangements of traditional German songs, but his chamber and orchestral music as well. His four symphonies are considered among the best of the Romantic period.

Brahms began studying piano when he was seven years old. As his talents developed, he accompanied several well-known Hungarian musicians in their tours around Europe. While still a young man, Brahms had the good fortune to be befriended by the German composers Robert and Clara Schumann, with whom he studied.

The *Academic Festival Overture* celebrates his receiving the honorary Doctor of Philosophy degree from the University of Breslau. He regarded the honor seriously, but the music that he composed almost pokes fun at the occasion! Using popular German tunes, he altered them slightly and constructed a serious orchestral piece from them.

Johannes Brahms   (1833–1897)

1. Opening theme begins in strings

2. Countermelody added by woodwinds and brass

3. Melody derived from "The Stately House"

4. Opening theme returns and crescendos

5. New theme begins in strings

6. Timpani roll followed by slow version of "The Stately House"

7. Opening theme returns

8. Fast fragments of "The Stately House"

9. Opening theme and countermelody

10. New theme introduced

11. New theme continues, preparing for "What Comes There O'er the Hill?"

12. Slow, ornamented version of "What Comes There O'er the Hill?"

13. Fast version of "What Comes There O'er the Hill?", then played in canon

14. New theme introduced

15. "What Comes There O'er the Hill?" using loud chords

16. Return of call 5 theme

17. Opening theme repeats, followed by fragments of all the themes

18. Coda — "Gaudeamus igitur" in a loud, strong ending

Vocal Style

How do you think this spiritual should be sung? Look at the melody line and the words. How can you use your voice to interpret this song in the best possible way?

Now Let Me Fly

African American Spiritual

A **REFRAIN** G
Now let me fly, _____ Now let me fly, _____

G
Now let me fly _____ way up high, _____

G   D₇   G   *Fine*
Way in the mid - dle of the air.

B **VERSE**
G
1. Way down yon - der in the mid - dle of the field,
2. I got a moth - er in the Prom - is'd _____ Land,

See me work - in' at the char - iot wheel.
Ain't gonna stop ___ 'til I shake her hand.

Not so par - tic - 'lar 'bout work - in' at the wheel, But I
Not so par - tic - 'lar 'bout shak - in' her ___ hand, But I

D.C. al Fine

just wan - na see how the char - iot feels.
just wan - na get up to the Prom - is'd Land.

Singing in Style

Here is another spiritual. Should it be performed in the same way as "Now Let Me Fly"? What kind of mood do the lyrics suggest?

Peace like a River

African American Spiritual   Arranged by Larry Eisman

1. I've got peace like a riv-er, I've got peace like a riv-er, I've got peace like a riv-er in my soul. _____ *(in my soul)* I've got peace like a riv-er, I've got peace like a riv-er, I've got peace _ like a riv-er in my soul. _____ *(in my soul)*

2. I've got joy like a fountain, . . .   3. I've got love like the ocean, . . .

Singing Styles

Singing well means singing a song in the style that is most appropriate. You can almost hear the style of singing when you look at these pictures of musicians in performance.

1. Placido Domingo
2. Arrested Development
3. The Bangles
4. Gloria Estefan
5. James Taylor
6. Dolly Parton

Musical interaction is like a musical conversation. It can sound like questions and answers, a lively debate, or even a friendly musical argument.

Look at "Long John." It follows a pattern of musical interaction known as **call and response**.

Musical Interaction

Long John

African American Blues Song

With his shin-y blade, _ *With his shin-y blade,* _ Got it in his hand, _ *Got it*

in his hand, _ Gon-na chop out the live oaks, *Gon-na chop out the live oaks,* That are

in this land. _ *That are in this land.* _ He's Long John, _ *He's Long John,* _ He's

long gone, _ *He's long gone,* _ He's gone, gone, _ *He's gone, gone,* _ Like a

tur - key in the corn, _ *Like a tur-key in the corn,* _ With his

long clothes on, _ *With his long clothes on,* _ He's long gone, _ *He's long gone,* _ He's

long gone, _ *He's long gone,* _ He's gone. *He's long gone.* _

A Diagram for Musical Interaction

Sometimes an instrument or voice sounds alone. Listen to this piece for solo violin.

 Sonata in G Minor for Unaccompanied Violin, "Presto" (excerpt) ....J. S. Bach

Use the symbol ✱ to represent one instrument or voice sounding alone.

More often, a number of instruments or voices will perform together. Listen to this string piece by Mozart.

 Eine kleine Nachtmusik, "Minuet" (excerpt) ....W. A. Mozart

Use the symbol ✱✱✱ for a group of instruments or voices.

In "Long John" the solo voice and the chorus take turns. Here is a way to show the interaction using the symbols above.

✱ ⟷ ✱✱✱

Hold 'em, Joe
Words and Music by Harry Thomas

Chorus

Hold 'em, Joe, Hold 'em, Joe, Hold 'em, Joe, but don't let him go.

Joe, but don't let him go. Me don - key want wa - ter, Hold 'em, Joe;

Spring 'round the cor - ner, Hold 'em, Joe; Me don - key want wa - ter, Hold 'em,

Joe; Ev - 'ry - bo - dy want wa - ter, Hold 'em, Joe; Fu - ma - la - ca tchim - ba,

Hold 'em, Joe; Me don - key want wa - ter, Hold 'em Joe; Ev - 'ry - bo - dy want

In "Long John" the call and response are exactly alike. The chorus simply echoes what it hears in the solo voice.

Often, however, the response is different. In this song, the group response of *Hold 'em, Joe* is different from the solo call.

wa - ter, Hold 'em Joe; Me don - key want wa - ter, Hold 'em, Joe. Hold 'em,

Joe, Hold 'em, Joe, Hold 'em, Joe, but don't let him go. Hold 'em,

Joe, but don't let him go. We on a jour - ney, he don't walk straight,

and that is ___ be - cause he's ___ so un - der - weight; That don - key ___ of

mine, he ___ don't like no weight, Put him on a cart and ___ he won't walk

straight. Me don - key want

Joe, but don't let him go!

More Call and Response

Are the responses the same as the calls in this song?

Michael, Row the Boat Ashore

African American Work Song

Call and Response for Instruments

Listen to a piece for solo trumpet and string instruments.

 Sonata in D for Trumpet and Strings, Mvt. 1
.............Henry Purcell

Which diagram best shows the musical interaction in this piece?

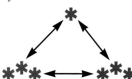

Now listen to this piece for solo guitar and orchestra.

 Fantasia para un gentilhombre, "Torch Dance"
................Joaquín Rodrigo

You can hear musical interaction among three groups.

1. Solo guitar
2. String section of the orchestra
3. Woodwind and brass sections of the orchestra

Notice how these three groups interact with each other. Which diagram above shows the call and response pattern for this piece?

Meet the Composer

Joaquín Rodrigo   (1901-   )

Blind since the age of 3, Spanish composer Joaquín Rodrigo began his music training while very young. He was interested mainly in composing, and had his first orchestral piece, *Juglares*, performed when he was only 23 years old. He studied composition throughout Europe during the 1920s and 30s. In 1940 his first piece for guitar and orchestra, *Concierto de Aranjuez*, made its very successful premiere. Rodrigo was soon regarded as one of Spain's leading contemporary composers.

He has received many awards during this century, including honorary doctorates, memberships, and medals of honor from many countries. His pieces for guitar and orchestra—such as the *Fantasia para un gentilhombre* which you have listened to—are performed and enjoyed throughout the world.

Sound Against Sound—
Antiphonal Music

Composers sometimes use one set of sounds alternating with another set of sounds. This is called **antiphonal** music.

You have probably guessed that call and response is one kind of antiphonal music. Another kind of antiphonal pattern can be called "group alternating with group."

 Echo Song ....di Lasso

Now listen to this piece by George Frideric Handel. It is an antiphonal piece for instruments, with three sets of instruments trading off. Sometimes one group will sound by itself, and sometimes two will sound at the same time. Once in a while they all play together.

 Water Music Suite, "Allegro" ....Handel

Listen to the piece again while you follow the printed score. Now you can *see* the musical interaction as well as hear it.

Water Music Suite
Allegro

G.F. Handel

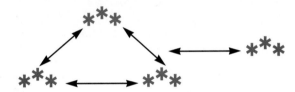

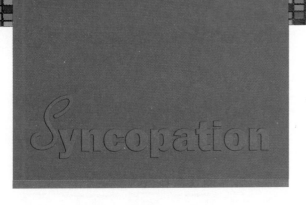

Syncopation

By now you are a master at keeping a steady beat! However, notes do not always fall on the beat. When notes begin before the beat, you have **syncopation**.

Try singing the version of "Didn't My Lord Deliver Daniel?" at the top of page 93. Not very exciting, is it? Now sing the real version. How does syncopation make a difference in the song?

Didn't My Lord Deliver Daniel?

African American Spiritual

Did - n't my Lord de - liv - er Dan - iel, __ de - liv - er

Dan - iel, __ de - liv - er Dan - iel? __ Did-n't my Lord de - liv - er

1. *First time only*

Dan - iel? __ Then why not - a ev - er - y man? Did - n't

Did-n't my Lord de - liv - er Dan - iel, de - liv - er

Dan - iel, de-liv-er Dan - iel? Did-n't my Lord de-liv - er

Dan - iel? Then why not - a ev - er - y man?

2. Em   Fine   **VERSE**   Am

man?   1. He de - liv - ered Dan - iel from the li - on's den, __
           2. Oh, the wind blows East ____ and the wind blows West, __
           3. When the moon run down ____ in a sil - ver stream, __

Em

Jo - nah from the bel - ly of the whale,   And the
Blows __ like a judge - a - ment __ day,   And __
Sun __ will re - fuse __ to __ shine,   And __

Am   Em

He - brew chil - dren from the fi - er - y fur - nace, then
ev - 'ry sin - ner who __ nev - er pray __ be
ev - 'ry star __ will __ dis - ap - pear, __ sal -

Em   Am   Em   D.S. al Fine

why not - a ev - er - y ____ man?   Did - n't
hap - py to pray on that __ day!   Did - n't
va - tion it will - a be ____ mine! Did - n't

Tying It Together

Sometimes syncopation occurs when a note is extended by a tie.

Where do the ties occur in this song from Puerto Rico?

Head for the Canefields　　(*Corta la caña*)

English Words by Aura Kontra　　*Folk Song from Puerto Rico*

I　work in the su - gar　cane _ fields,　The　crop that I bear is heav -
Yo　ven-go de mon-te a-den - tro　de　cor - tar ca-ña, ca - ñe -

- y,　No　mat-ter how much I car - ry　it will　nev - er bring much mon -
- ro,　por más ca - ña　que se cor - te nun-ca　se　ga-na el　di - ne -

- ey.　Some say　it's an ea-sy liv - ing,　cut - ting su-gar　all day
- ro.　To - do el mun-do la pro - cla - ma　que es muy fá - cil　de cor -

94 **Rhythm**

long.   When-ev-er   a hand is need - ed   no one   wants to come a-long.
tar,   *cuan-do se   ja-la   la mo - cha na-die   quie-re   tra-ba-jar.*

Head for the cane - fields each morn-ing,   cut   them   down. _
Cor - ta   la   ca - ña,   ca - ñe - ro,   cór - ta - la. ____

Head for the cane - fields till   sun - set,   cut   them   down. _
Cor - ta   la   ca - ña,   ca - ñe - ro,   cór - ta - la. ____

Can you hear the syncopation in this Cuban
guajira, also about cutting sugarcane?

*Tumba la caña.......*José Rodriguez

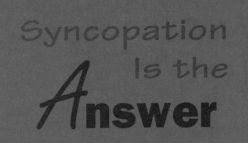

Syncopation Is the Answer

Where does the syncopation occur in this song?

The Answer Lies in You and in Me

Words and Music by Cici Hunt

VERSE

1. So ma-ny child-ren — are walk-ing a-lone. — They
2. Let's work to-ge - ther, — it's our world to share. . Come
3. Let's work to-ge - ther, — we can if we try. —

walk a-fraid — with-out a place to call their own. —
on, you'll see — what hap-pens when we learn to care. —
Then we'll all — be bus-y 'stead of ask-ing "why?" —

We may be dif - f'rent, — but one thing is clear; — please
We need each oth - er — the need is so clear; — just
Let's help our neigh - bor, — we know that we can; — come

lis-ten, here's a song, it's for the whole world to hear. ——
take a look a-round, you'll see the an - swer is here. ——
on now, let's reach out and give a help - ing hand. ——

REFRAIN

Let's make a dif-f'rence, _ we can if we try, _ Child-ren are hurt-ing, _ we

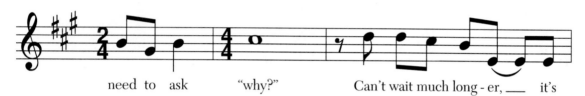

need to ask "why?" Can't wait much long - er, ___ it's

Last time to Coda ⊕ | 1., 2.   **3**

our world, you see, _ the an-swer lies in you and in me. _

3. (repeat refrain only)   ⊕ *Coda*

an - swer lies in you and in me.   an - swer lies in you and in me. _

rit.

_ The an-swer lies in you and in me.

Dots — an Uneven Rhythm

When you want to add a little flavor to a rhythm pattern, syncopation is a great technique to use. Another alternative is to use **dotted rhythms.**

Start with a chant using a sixteenth-note pattern.

dah   dah   dah   dee   dah   dah   dah   dee

Now chant just the first and last sound in each group.

dah _____ dee   dah _____ dee

There is an easier way to write this rhythm pattern. You can find it in the song "Do, Lord."

dah   dee   dah   dee

Try adding this rhythm accompaniment once you have learned the song.

Clap

End with

Tambourine

shake   hit   hit

Do, Lord

African American Spiritual

REFRAIN

Do, Lord, oh do, Lord, oh do re-mem-ber me,   Do, Lord, oh do, Lord,

oh do re-mem-ber me.   Do, Lord, oh do, Lord, oh do re-mem-ber me,

rit. last time   Look a - way   be - yond ___ the blue.

VERSE

I got a home in glo - ry land that   out - shines the sun,

I got a home in glo - ry land that   out - shines the sun.

I got a home in glo - ry land that   out - shines the sun,

Look a - way   be - yond ___ the blue.

Dotted Rhythm in Six

The dotted pattern you learned in "Do, Lord" was based on four notes. Here is a new pattern based on six notes—a meter in 6. You can learn it the same way.

DAH dah DAH dah DEE dah DAH dah DAH dah DEE dah

Leavin' for Chile   (Cuando pa' Chile me voy)

English Words by Aura Kontra   *Cueca from Chile*

1. Leav - in' for Chi - le   a - gain,   I'm cross-ing the high-est moun-tains.
   And when I come home from Chi - le,   I cross o - ver hills and riv - ers.
   Cuan-do pa' Chi - le   me voy,   Cru-zan - do la cor - di - lle - ra,
   Y   cuan-do vuel - vo   de Chi - le,   En - tre ce-rros y que-bra - das,

moun-tains. And my   hap-py heart is   sing-ing,   for some-one I know there is
riv - ers. And my   hap-py heart is   sing-ing,   for soon I'll be court - ing an -
lle - ra, La-te el   co - ra-zón con - ten - to,   Pues u - na chi - le - na me es-
bra - das, La-te el   co - ra-zón con - ten - to,   Pues me es-pe-ra u - na cu -

REFRAIN

wait - ing. And my   wait - ing.   Long live the mu-sic of the dan-za, long live the
oth - er. And my   oth - er.   *Vi - van el bai-le y la dan-za, vi - van la*
pe - ra. La-te el   pe - ra.
ya - na. La-te el   ya - na.

Now omit the the second, third, and sixth notes in each group.

DAH ___ dah DEE _ DAH ___ dah DEE _

You are left with this pattern.

DAH   dah DEE   DAH   dah DEE

After you have learned "Leavin' for Chile," listen to a different version of the song as performed by the South American group Andes Manta.

Cuando pa' Chile me voy
..............Cueca from Chile

cue - ca and zam - ba.   At jour-ney's end or at jour-ney's be - gin-ning,
cue - ca y la zam - ba,   *Dos pun - tas tie-ne el ca - mi - no y en las dos*

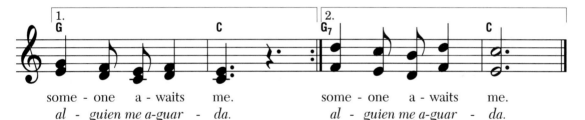

some - one   a - waits   me.   some - one   a - waits   me.
al - guien me a-guar - da.   *al - guien me a-guar - da.*

2. I dance the cueca in Chile, ⎫ *2 times*
    In Cuyo I do the zamba.   ⎭
    Dancing with the girls from Chile, ⎫ *2 times*
    Or with the ones from Calingasta. ⎭
    Days can be happy or sad, ⎫ *2 times*
    The life of an *arriero*.   ⎭
    Troubles face me on my journey, ⎫ *2 times*
    But laughter awaits me at nightfall. ⎭

    Refrain

2. *En Chile bailo la cueca,* ⎫ *2 times*
    En Cuyo bailo la zamba, ⎭
    En Chile con las chilenas, ⎫ *2 times*
    Con las otras en Calingasta. ⎭
    Vida trist, vida alegre, ⎫ *2 times*
    Es la vida del arriero, ⎭
    Penitas en el camino,   ⎫ *2 times*
    Y risas al fin del sendero. ⎭

    Refrain

Major and Minor Scales

Here is a **scale** with the note C as its tonal center.

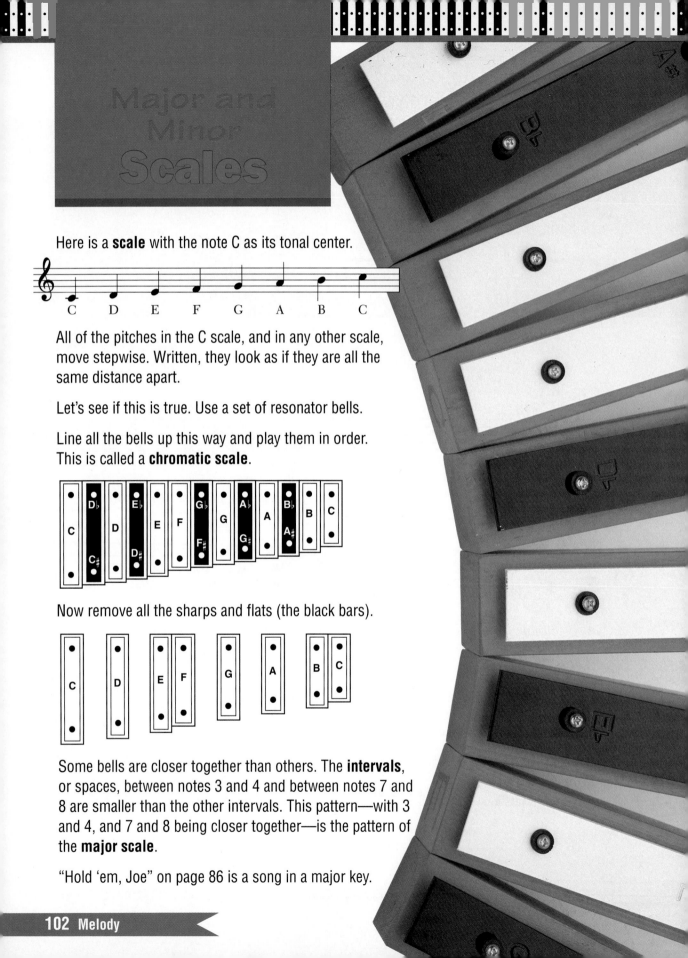

C D E F G A B C

All of the pitches in the C scale, and in any other scale, move stepwise. Written, they look as if they are all the same distance apart.

Let's see if this is true. Use a set of resonator bells.

Line all the bells up this way and play them in order. This is called a **chromatic scale**.

Now remove all the sharps and flats (the black bars).

Some bells are closer together than others. The **intervals**, or spaces, between notes 3 and 4 and between notes 7 and 8 are smaller than the other intervals. This pattern—with 3 and 4, and 7 and 8 being closer together—is the pattern of the **major scale**.

"Hold 'em, Joe" on page 86 is a song in a major key.

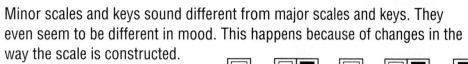

Minor scales and keys sound different from major scales and keys. They even seem to be different in mood. This happens because of changes in the way the scale is constructed.

Set up the bells as you did before for the C major scale. Replace E with E♭, A with A♭, and B with B♭.

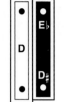

The interval between notes 2 and 3 and between notes 5 and 6 is smaller than the other intervals. Notice that the interval between 6 and 7 is larger than the others. This kind of minor scale is called **natural minor**.

Listen to this familiar round. It is in a major key.

 Are You Sleeping? (major)..........Traditional

Notice how different it sounds in a minor key.

 Are You Sleeping? (minor)..........Traditional

Mix It Up!

Sometimes composers use both major *and* minor scales as the framework for the melody. In this song, the tonal center stays the same but the change in key signature tells you that something different will happen between the verse and the refrain.

El capotín

English Words by Aura Kontra   *Folk Song from Puerto Rico*

Turn 'round and see _____ what I've brought, pret - ty
Yo te da - ré, _____ te da - ré, ni - ña her-

la - dy, Can you guess what I'm hid - ing? ____ It's a
mo - sa, Te da - ré un - a co - sa, _____ un - a

cup of hot cof - fee for you. Sur - prise!
co - sa que yo só - lo sé: ¡Ca - fe!

Sing a ca - po - tín, tín, tín, tín, tín, tín, tín, { there's a / did you
Con el ca - po - tín, tín, tín, tín, tín, tín, tín, { es - ta / es - ta

chance it will rain ___ to - night.
know that to - night it will snow?
no - che va a llo - ver.
no - che va a ne - var.

Sing a ca - po -
Con el ca - po -

tín, tín, tín, tín, tín, tín, tín, { it will start in the
{ it will fall in the

tín, tín, tín, tín, tín, tín, tín, { *a e - so del a -*
{ *a e - so de la*

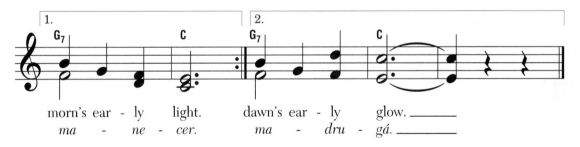

1.
morn's ear - ly light.
ma - ne - cer.

2.
dawn's ear - ly glow. ___
ma - dru - gá. ___

The Czechoslovakian composer Antonín Dvořák used major and minor scales in this exciting dance. It is very fast—can you hear the alternating tonalities?

Slavonic Dance No. 8, Op. 46 ....Antonín Dvořák

Pentatonic Scales

Major and minor scales use eight different pitches. The first and last pitches of these scales have the same name.

There are other scales that have less than eight pitches. A **pentatonic** scale has only five.

Asadoya

Folk Song from Okinawa

1. Ah, House of As - a - do - ya, ___ Why are you so dear to ___
2. A - las ___ fair Ku - ya - ma, ___ Cru - el, o cru - el was

me? Sa yu - i yu - i, 'Tis where Ku - ya - ma
she, Sa yu - i yu - i, Cold - ly dis - dain - ing me,

Here are the five different notes that are used in the song below.

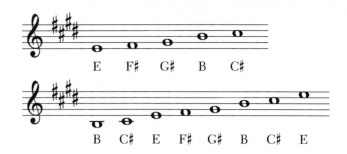

E   F♯   G♯   B   C♯

Some of these pitches are repeated in higher or lower registers. Here is the entire range of "Asadoya."

B   C♯   E   F♯   G♯   B   C♯   E

first the light of day __ did __ see. And she was my love, my
She re-fused my bride _ to __ be. And she was my love, my

dar - ling, and all the world to me. _____
dar - ling, and all the world to me. _____

3. Lo! now I have wed another,
   Fairer by far than thee.
   Sa yui yui,
   With graceful manners fine,
   Dwell we now in happy harmony,
   And she is my love, my darling,
      and all the world to me.

4. And if she bear me a son,
   Ruler of this town he will be;
   Sa yui yui,
   And if a daughter fair,
   A model of sweet felicity,
   And she'll be my love, my darling,
      and all the world to me.

Listen to this Japanese instrumental piece, written hundreds of years ago. Very few notes are used to create the melody. Do the notes create a pentatonic scale?

Entenraku
..........Art Piece from Japan

Music from China

Here is another song that is based on a pentatonic scale. Look carefully at the song and see if you can determine which five different pitches are used.

A Boat on the Lake (Tai-hu)

Folk Song from China *Collected by Shao-Mei Ting*

Wind   is   blow - ing   a - cross   the __ lake,   Qui - et - ly ____ the
Shan ching sho - ei ming iuo   jing __ jing,   hu   shin   peau __ lai
shahn cheeng sho - ay meeng yo   jeeng   jeeng   hoo   shin   payau   lahee

rip - ples __ play;   We   row   and __ row,   we   row   and __ row.
feng   i ____ jehn,   a   shyng   a ____ shyng   a,   jihn   a ____ jihn,
fung   ee   jehn   ah   sheeng ah   sheeng   ah   jin   ah   jin

Few   there   are   who walk   by   the shore,   Where the   lake __ re -
hwang   huen shyr   hau   ren   shyng __ shao,   baun kong   yu - eh ying
wahng   wehn sheer   hau   rehn sheeng   shau   baun kawng yoo - eh yeeng

flects   the __ moon;   We   row   and __ row,   we   row   and __ row.
shoei   mi - an yau,   a   shyng   a ____ shyng   a,   jihn   a ____ jihn.
shoay mee-ahn yau   ah   sheeng ah   sheeng   ah   jin   ah   jin

Purple Bamboo Melody............Traditional Piece from China

Ni Tsan. Woods and Valleys of Mount Yu. The Metropolitan Museum of Art, Gift of The Dillion Fund, 1973.

Hanging Scroll *Ni Tsan*

On page 103 you listened to two versions of *Are You Sleeping?* —one in major and the other in minor. Here is how that song would sound and look based on a pentatonic scale.

Are You Sleeping? (pentatonic) ....Traditional

Something New!

During the turn of this century, some composers began using a new kind of scale with no half steps—only whole steps. This new scale became known as the **whole-tone** scale. Because it has no half steps, it has a distant, dreamy feel to it.

Here is *Are You Sleeping?* as it would sound and look using a whole-tone scale.

Are You Sleeping? (whole tone) ....Traditional

Singing in *Harmony*

Try singing this popular Mexican song in two parts. The harmony part is an interval of a third above the melody.

Las mañanitas

English Words by Lupe Allegria   *Folk Song from Mexico*

Guitar: capo 3

Hear us sing *las ma - ña - ni - tas* as the
Es - tas son las ma - ña - ni - tas Que can -

morn - ing light ap - pears, And the gen - tle bird will
ta - ba el Rey Da - vid, A las mu - cha - chas bo -

join in the hap - py mu - sic he hears. Oh,
ni - tas Se las can - ta - mos a - quí. Des -

Listen to this beautiful song for two voices. It is part of a larger work composed by Andrew Lloyd Webber.

First you will hear each voice singing a solo melody. Later they will sing a duet in thirds.

Requiem, "Pie Jesu"
.............Andrew Lloyd Webber

wake up and see the sun - shine. Oh, wake up and meet the
pier - ta, mi bien, des - pier - ta, Mi - ra que ya a-man - ne -

day. Hear, the morn - ing bird is sing - ing, the sil - ver
ció; Ya los pa - ja - ri - llos can - tan, La lu - na

moon has gone a - way.
ya ___ se me - tió.

1. Instrumental introduction
2. Woman soprano solo
3. Boy soprano solo
4. Woman sings melody—boy harmonizes in thirds
5. Interlude (using melody from introduction)
6. Woman and boy sing duet
7. Coda (using melody from introduction)

Call Chart

Spanish American music often uses harmonies based on thirds and sixths. Notice how both types are used in "Springtime."

Springtime   *(La primavera)*

English Words by Linda Williams   *Spanish Folk Song from California*

At   last comes the   spring,   the   sea - son   so _____ full   of
Ya   vie - ne   la   pri -   ma - ve - ra,   sem   -   bran - do

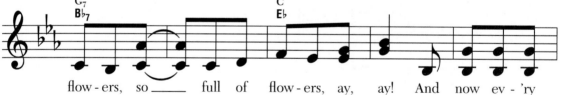

flow - ers,   so _____ full   of   flow - ers,   ay,   ay!   And   now   ev - 'ry
flo - res,   sem   - bran - do   flo - res,   ay,   ay!   Y   ya   los   cam -

field   is   paint - ed   so _____ man - y   col - ors,   so _____ man - y
pos   se es - mal - tan   de _____ mil   co - lo - res,   de _____ mil   co -

When two or more pitches sound at the same time, they form a **chord**. When you strike a combination of keys on the piano, or strum several strings at once on the guitar, you are playing a chord.

You can create chords with resonator bells.

Make a three-note chord to play on the bells.

Make another chord, using different bells.

Add one more chord and you can play an accompaniment for "Las mañanitas" on page 110.

Chord Progressions

As you harmonize with chords, you will notice that your ear tells you when you need to change from one chord to another. This changing pattern in the harmony is called the **chord progression**.

Many songs we like to sing have interesting but simple chord progressions. The most commonly used chords are the ones based on the first, fourth, and fifth notes in the scale. We use Roman numerals (I, IV, V) to identify the chords.

In the key of G, those three chords look like this.

Most of the songs in this book have chord names above the melody.

Using the chords illustrated above, add an instrument and harmonize with the chords. Then play an accompaniment for the partner songs on pages 36 and 37.

Putting it all Together

Here is a song that uses only three chords in its harmonic progression. For a challenge, create an accompaniment using the three chords found in "The Cowpoke": F (I), B♭ (IV), and C (V).

Here is a rhythm you might use on autoharp or bells.

Try this rhythm on xylophones or keyboard.

Now add some percussion.

To make your accompaniment complete, add this countermelody using a melody instrument.

The Cowpoke (El payo)

English Words by Alice Firgau   *Folk Song from Mexico*

Guitar: capo 3

1. Oh, Nick, a sad, old cow-poke, Would sit all day on a fence.
   Es - ta-ba un pa - yo sen - ta - do En tran-cas de un co - rral;

The fore-man saw him and told him, "Your sad-ness does-n't make sense."
Y el ma - yor - do - mo le di - jo, "No es-tés tris - te, Ni - co - lás."

"Just give me all that I ask for And you'd cheer my low mor - ale."
"Si quie - res que no es-té tris-te Lo que pi - da me has de dar."

The fore-man smiled then and told him, "Well, start ask-ing, Nick, old pal."
Y el ma - yor - do - mo le di - jo, "Ve pi - dien-do, Ni - co - lás."

2. "I need some thirty *pesos*,
   A jacket, coat, and a hat."
   The foreman smiled then and told him,
   "No money have I for that."
   "I need those thirty *pesos*
   For to marry my sweet gal."
   The foreman smiled then and told him,
   "I have none, my dear, old pal."

2. *"Necesito treinta pesos,*
   Una cuera y un gabán."
   Y el mayordomo le dijo,
   "No hay dinero, Nicolás."
   "Necesito treinta pesos
   Para poderme casar."
   Y el mayordomo le dijo,
   "Ni un real tengo, Nicolás."

An Instrumental Style

You have learned how musical styles have changed over the centuries. Some traditions have been maintained by composers, whereas others have been replaced altogether. In a way, music is a little like clothing—fads come and go, but truly classic styles last forever!

Listen to this movement from a piano piece by Judith Lang Zaimont. The composer used traditional holiday carols as themes and developed them using a contemporary style.

A Calendar Set, "December" ....Judith Lang Zaimont

1. Introduction (suggesting chimes and bells)

2. *O Come, All Ye Faithful* - in canon between left and right hands

3. *God Rest Ye Merry, Gentlemen* - slow, with melody and rhythm fragmented

4. Last phrase of *God Rest Ye Merry, Gentlemen*

5. *Joy to the World* - forte

6. *Bring a Torch, Jeannette, Isabella* - piano and legato

7. *Bring a Torch, Jeannette, Isabella* - fast, interrupted by *God Rest Ye Merry, Gentlemen*

8. *God Rest Ye Merry, Gentlemen* - accented, forte, and fast

9. *Silent Night* - fortissimo with rapidly descending scales

10. *Deck the Halls* - fast

11. *Joy to the World* - accented and forte

12. *God Rest Ye Merry, Gentlemen* - legato and getting softer

Meet the Composer

Judith Lang Zaimont (1945-)

Born in Memphis, Tennessee, Judith Lang Zaimont grew up in New York City. Music was important to her family, and she began studying piano with her mother at age five. She started composing at eleven, the same year she began studies at the Juilliard School of Music. She won national prizes for a piano suite and a flute sonata that she wrote before she was fifteen years old.

Zaimont is known not only for her piano and choral compositions but also for her works for orchestra, chamber ensemble, dance, film, and opera. She often uses different cultural styles in her music, such as Native American and Eskimo themes.

She has won many prizes for her music. Her works have been performed on four continents, and also on television and radio. An active teacher of composition, she is also a writer on musical subjects. She is the author of *The Musical Woman*, a book series on women musicians.

Styles of Different Cultures

A Native American Style

This song was written by two Native American college students. The harmonies in the song are similar to those we are used to hearing in popular music. However, the melody and words echo the heritage of the songwriters. The lyrics tell of looking to tribal leaders for guidance and inspiration, as Native Americans have for many centuries.

You can learn to perform "Go, My Son" in traditional Native American sign language. Use the signs illustrated on pages 122 and 123.

Go, My Son

Words and Music by Burson-Nofchissey

Spoken: *Long ago an Indian war chief counseled his people in the ways that they should walk. He wisely told them that education is the ladder to success and happiness. "Go, my son, and climb that ladder. . . ."*

1. Go, my son,   go and climb the lad - der. Go, my son,
2. Work, my son,   get an ed - u - ca - tion. Work, my son,
     on the lad - der   of an ed - u - ca - tion, You can see to

go and earn your fea - ther.   Go, my son,   make your peo - ple proud of
learn a good vo - ca - tion and climb, my son,   go and take a loft - y
help your In - dian na - tion and reach, my son, and lift your peo - ple up with

you. _____

view. _____ 3. From

you. _____

Go, my son,   go and climb the lad - der. Go, my son,
on the lad - der of an ed - u - ca - tion, You can see to

Last time to Coda

go and earn your fea - ther.   Go my son,   make your peo-ple proud of
help your In - dian na - tion, and

you. _____ From reach, my son,   Lift your peo-ple up with you.

Signing
a Native American Song

Here are the signs you can use as you sing "Go, My Son."

climb

proud

good

vocation

of you

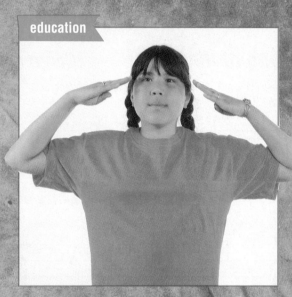

education

Indian

reach

Now listen to some traditional Native American music. In this excerpt, the only tones you will hear are the five notes of a pentatonic scale.

Look at the melody of "Go, My Son." How is it similar to the *Round Dance Song*?

Round Dance Song (excerpt)
...............Traditional Taos

A South American Style

"Song of the Water" is a *joropo*, a type of song and dance that originated in the central plains region of Venezuela. This lyrical *joropo* tells of a singer performing an early morning song to his beloved by the banks of a river.

Song of the Water (Canto del agua)

English Words by Alice Firgau   *Joropo from Venezuela*

1. You can hear me sing a love song _____ as I
Es un can-to ma-ña-ne-ro _____ a la o-

stand be-side the riv - er. _____ You can hear me sing a
ri - lli - ta del rí - o, _____ Es un can-to ma - ña-

love song _____ as I stand be-side the riv - er. In the
ne - ro _____ a la o - ri - lli - ta del rí - o, Que te

ear - ly morn-ing hours, feel-ing cold, I sing and shiv - er. In the
va di - cien - do, ne - gra, tá - pa - me que ten - go frí - o. Que te

8

ear-ly morn-ing hours, feel-ing cold, I sing and shiv - er.
va di-cien - do, ne - gra, tá - pa - me que ten - go frí - o. _____

An Asian Style

This well-known song from Vietnam involves antiphonal group singing, or *quan ho.* One of the most respected folk traditions in Vietnam, *quan ho* often occurs during spring and autumn harvesting festivals. Participants dress in their finest, most traditional costumes to represent their villages, and throughout the days of preparation build friendships with other singers.

The Wind on the Bridge   (Quâ Cầu Gió Bay)

Folk Song from Vietnam

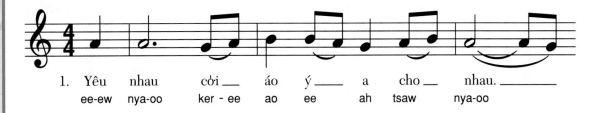

1. Yêu   nhau   cởi __ áo   ý __ a   cho __ nhau. _____
ee-ew   nya-oo   ker - ee   ao   ee   ah   tsaw   nya-oo

Về __ nhà   dối __ rằng   cha   dối __ mẹ __ a   ý __ a.
vay   nyah   zoh - ee   zang   tsah   zoh - ee   mae   ah   ee   ah

Rằng   a   ý __ a __ qua   cầu.   Rằng   a   ý __ a __ qua   cầu.
zang   ah   ee   ah   kwa   kah-oo   zang   ah   ee   ah   kwa   ka-oo

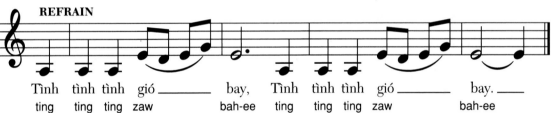

Tình   tình tình gió ——————— bay,   Tình   tình tình gió ——————— bay. ———
ting   ting ting zaw   bah-ee ting   ting ting zaw   bah-ee

2. Yêu nhau cởi nón ý a cho nhau.
    ee-ew nya-oo ker-ee nawn ee ah tsaw nya-oo
    Về nhà dối rằng cha dối mẹ a ý a.
    vay nyah zoh-ee zang tsah zoh-ee mae ah ee ah
    Rằng a ý a qua cầu. Rằng a ý a qua cầu.
    zang ah ee ah kwa ka-oo

3. Yêu nhau cởi nhẫn ý a cho nhau.
    ee-ew nya-oo ker-ee nyern ee ah tsaw nya-oo
    Về nhà dối rằng cha dối mẹ a ý a.
    vay nyah zoh-ee zang tsah zoh-ee mae ah ee ah
    Rằng a ý a qua cầu. Rằng a ý a qua cầu.
    zang ah ee ah kwa ka-oo

Final Refrain: Tình tình tình đánh rơi,
                ting ting ting dah-n zer-ee
                Tình tình tình đánh rơi.
                ting ting ting dah-n zer-ee

An African American Style

We learned how the USA for Africa organization, along with many other groups, worked together to lend a helping hand to African nations during a severe drought.

Lean on Me

Words and Music by Bill Withers

1. Some - times in our lives __ we all have pain, __ we all have
2. Please swal-low your pride __ if I have things __ you need to
3. If there is a load __ you have to bear __ that you can't

sor - row. __ But if we are wise __ we know that there's __
bor - row, __ For no one can fill ___ those of your needs __
car - ry, ___ I'm right up the road. __ I'll share your load __

__ al -ways to - mor - row.
__ that you won't let ___ show. } Lean on me ___ when you're not strong _
__ if you just call __ me.

__ and I'll be your friend, _ I'll help you car - ry on, __

For it won't be long __ till I'm gon-na need _ some-bod-y to lean _

Sometimes help is needed on a smaller scale. Whenever our friends need help, we try to be there to show our support. It helps to have someone listen to us and be willing to share our problems.

After you sing this modern arrangement of "Lean on Me," listen to the original version as performed by the composer.

 Lean on Me.............Bill Withers

____ on. _ ____ on. _ Just call on me, broth-er, when

you need a hand. _ We all _ need some-bod-y to lean _____ on. I just

might have a prob-lem that you'd un-der-stand. _ We all _ need some-bod-y to lean _

____ on. Lean on me _ when you're not strong ___ and I'll be your friend, _

_ I'll help you car - ry on, _ For it won't be long _

till I'm gon-na need _ some-bod-y to lean _____ on. _

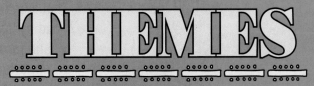

THEMES

Your trek across the globe continues,
but you will now travel back in time as well.

In this section of your book, you will see
how music has influenced and helped shape
the many cultures of the world.
Think about the following as you journey on.

What role did music have in
early civilizations?

Does every culture have a
music tradition?

How has our culture
been influenced by music?

section 2

The Turn of the Century

The arrival of the twentieth century brought many changes to the United States. New ideas were being explored in science. New technology was being utilized in industry. Women were fighting for equal rights, beginning with the right to vote. People throughout the world watched the United States change. Some decided that a better life could be had by leaving their homeland for this new land of opportunity.

The World Emigrates

Immigrants from many countries have come to these shores over the years, bringing their customs, languages, and songs. Many still come today seeking opportunity in the United States.

*M*eet the *C*omposer

George Gershwin   (1898–1937)

George Gershwin's life was tragically short, but his impact on American music was great. He wrote such famous songs as "I Got Rhythm," "Liza," and "Strike Up the Band." Many of his songs have become popular classics. His compositions for musical theater are among his most famous and best-loved pieces. His opera, *Porgy and Bess*, is considered by many to be his finest work.

Gershwin also wrote serious concert pieces, using the catchy melodies, jazzy harmonies, and driving rhythms of popular music. You are probably familiar with some of Gershwin's concert pieces, such as *Rhapsody in Blue*. They are played all over the world, and have been recorded by many famous orchestras and concert artists.

You may already have heard Gershwin's most famous work, *Rhapsody in Blue*. The opening clarinet glissando immediately announces that the piece will be full of **jazz** elements.

 Rhapsody in Blue (excerpt) ....Gershwin

In *An American in Paris*, Gershwin drew a musical picture of a visitor to Paris walking the busy streets.

 An American in Paris (excerpts) ....Gershwin

Africa Comes to America

With the coming of the new century, new musical styles that were distinctively American were born. Ragtime, a style mostly used for piano, is African American in origin. It is characterized by a syncopated melody line with a steady, on-the-beat bass line. Ragtime had a profound influence not only on Gershwin's writing, but on other composers and musical styles around the world.

Listen to these three rags, each performed by the composer. Though they differ in style, all have that ragtime rhythm!

Pineapple Rag (excerpt) ....Scott Joplin

Root Beer Rag (excerpt) ....Billy Joel

Reflective Rag (excerpt) ....Judy Zaimont

A Rag Song

Irving Berlin is another American composer who was influenced by ragtime. One of his best-known songs is "Alexander's Ragtime Band." It is a rag song—a popular song style made famous by Berlin that used ragtime rhythms.

Alexander's Ragtime Band

Words and Music by Irving Berlin   *Arranged by Carmen Culp and Don Kalbach*

Countermelody

Come on and hear, come on and hear Al - ex-

Melody

Come on and hear, come on and hear Al - ex-

an - der's Rag-time Band. Come on and hear,

an - der's Rag-time Band. Come on and hear, come on and

Selling One's Songs

A composer of this era would typically take a job as a song plugger—a slang term for a songwriter who worked for a music publisher. A song plugger also had to perform his or her songs to convince other musicians to use them.

Gershwin's first hit was a song called "Swanee," written in 1919. It sold over 200,000 records, giving him a status similar to that of a rock star today!

Swanee

Words by Irving Caesar   *Music by George Gershwin*

Guitar:

Swan - ee, How I love you, How I love you, My dear old Swan-ee; ___

I'd give the world to be A-mong the folks in D - I - X - I -

E - ven now there's some - one Wait-ing for me, Pray-ing for me

Down by the Swan-ee, ___ The folks up north will

see me no more ___ When I get to the Swan-ee shore. ___

The _European_ Connection

In addition to being one of America's foremost composers, George Gershwin was an accomplished pianist. He wrote many works for solo piano, both popular and serious.

One of the more classical forms in which Gershwin wrote was the prelude. As the name implies, preludes are short instrumental pieces that usually come before another movement or section of a larger work. During the Romantic era in Europe, however, composers began to write preludes that were to be played either separately or with other preludes.

Call Chart

Listen to these piano preludes from three different centuries. Notice how they are alike and how they are different.

1. Even rhythms, broken chords, one mood throughout

 The Well-Tempered Clavier, "Prelude No. 1" ....J. S. Bach

2. Thick texture, rich harmony, block chords

 Prelude No. 20, Op. 28 ....Frederic Chopin

3. Rhythms and harmonies often found in jazz; melody in the style of popular music

 Three Piano Preludes, "Prelude No. 2" ....George Gershwin

Jazz in a Larger Work

Composers throughout the world, particularly in the United States, were greatly influenced by ragtime and jazz styles during the 1920s. When Gershwin was in his early twenties, he began to use his jazzy, syncopated melodies in writing larger musical works. He wrote the famous *Rhapsody in Blue* in 1924 and his *Concerto in F* a year later. Although both pieces are for traditional orchestra and piano, they were considered anything *but* traditional at the time!

Listen to the main themes of the third movement from *Concerto in F.*

Concerto in F, Themes from Movement 3............George Gershwin

4. **D**

5. **E**

6. **B**

7. Coda

Concerto in F, Movement 3.............George Gershwin

Syncopation—the *Key Element*

You have learned that ragtime and jazz styles are characterized by syncopated rhythms. Syncopation adds a lot of energy to music, but it can be very tricky to perform.

Look at the rhythm grid below. It shows you step by step how to prepare for the syncopation found in Gershwin's classic song "I Got Rhythm." Start by tapping the rhythm in line 1. Once you have mastered one line, go on to the next. By the time you get to line 7, you've got the rhythm!

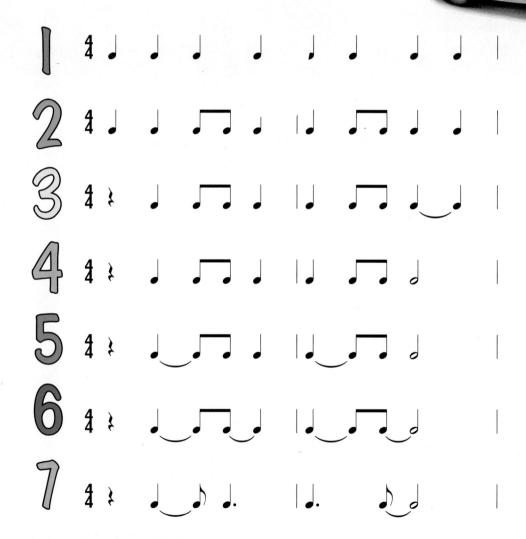

I Got Rhythm

Words by Ira Gershwin Music by George Gershwin

I ___ got rhy - thm, ___ I ___ got mu - sic, ___
I ___ got dai - sies ___ In ___ green pas - tures, ___

I ___ got my man, ___ Who could ask for an - y-thing more?
I ___ got my man, ___ Who could ask for an - y-thing more?

Old ___ Man Trou - ble, ___ I ___ don't mind him, ___ You ___ won't

find him ___ 'Round ___ my door, I ___ got star - light, ___

I ___ got sweet dreams, ___ I ___ got my man, ___ who could

ask for an - y-thing more, Who could ask for an - y-thing more?

Now listen to this recording of the original piano arrangement.

I Got Rhythm ....George Gershwin

Bands— A World Tradition

Bands have existed for thousands of years. Nearly every society in every part of the world has some tradition of group playing. There were bands even before there was a system for writing down music. These early bands probably consisted of trumpets and drums and were used for military ceremonies and for signals during battle.

During the Middle Ages and the Renaissance in Europe, each town had a band. These town bands probably played for community events as well as for military parades.

Ceremonies and Celebrations

Through the ages, the sound of wind and percussion instruments has signaled important events and ceremonies. Fanfares—bright-sounding trumpet calls—have been played to introduce important people or proclamations.

 La péri, "Overture" (excerpt).............Paul Dukas

Bands are used by cultures throughout the world for all kinds of occasions. Listen to the bright, lively sound of this mariachi band from Mexico.

 La leva.................Folk Song from Mexico

Even in concert, a marching band can make a stirring, exciting sound rarely found in other kinds of music. Probably the most famous American band composer was John Philip Sousa. His marches have become concert and parade favorites all over the world.

Semper Fidelis ....John Philip Sousa

Meet the Composer

John Philip Sousa is known as the March King of the world. He was born and grew up in our nation's capital—Washington, D.C. Even as a little boy, he knew he wanted to be a musician. He often went to band rehearsals with his father, who played trombone in the United States Marine Band—the official band of the President of the United States. When Sousa was 26 years old, he became director of this band and wrote some of his finest marches for it.

Sousa composed more than one hundred marches during his lifetime. Many of these are played today by high school, college, and community bands throughout America.

John Philip Sousa
(1854–1932)

A circus is a perfect place to have a band—especially to whip up excitement in the audience. That's exactly what this song from the musical *Barnum* is intended to do.

A Band on Broadway

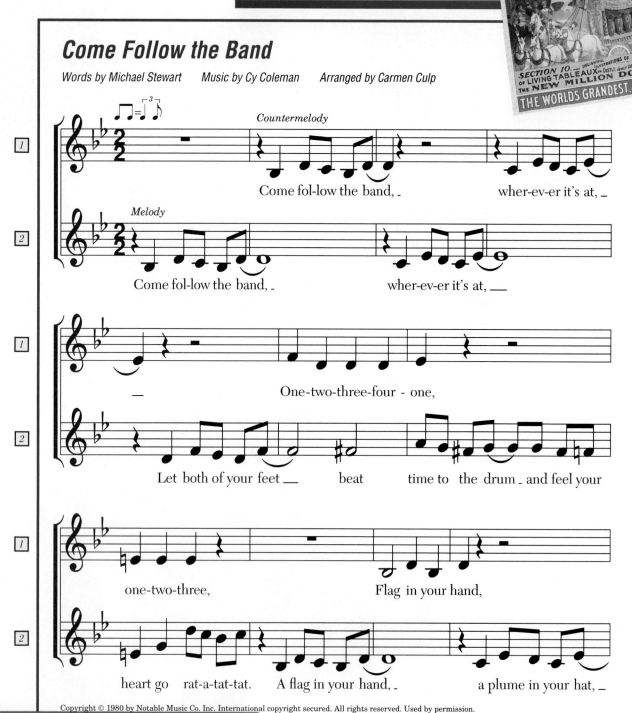

Come Follow the Band

Words by Michael Stewart   Music by Cy Coleman   Arranged by Carmen Culp

Countermelody

Come fol-low the band, ___ wher-ev-er it's at, ___

Melody

Come fol-low the band, ___ wher-ev-er it's at, ___

___ One-two-three-four - one,

Let both of your feet ___ beat time to the drum ___ and feel your

one-two-three, Flag in your hand,

heart go rat-a-tat-tat. A flag in your hand, ___ a plume in your hat, ___

big bass drum go by. __ Ain't you glad that you stayed? Boom Boom.

big bass drum go by. __ Ain't you glad that you stayed?

Oom- pah - pah, oom - pah - pah,

Hear the tu - ba play that oom-pah - pah, oh my, __ ain't it driv-in' you

cra - zy oom-pah - pah. Oom-pah oom-pah - pah,

cra - zy? __ Don't you be so darn la - zy, __

Join that big par - ade. __

Bet-ter hur - ry and join that big par - ade. __ Up out - a your seat, __

Band Music from Italy

Bands are an important part of American culture. Many other countries have similar band traditions. Here is one example from Italy. How do people regard the drummer of the band in this song?

The Band from Assori (Il tamburo della banda d'Assori)

English Words by Stefano Carbini and Giorgio Gentiluomo   *Traditional Song from Italy*

They're march-ing a - long, they're march-ing a-long, they're march-ing a-
Ar - ri - va la ban - da, ar - ri - va la ban - da, ar - ri - va la

long with a mer - ry song. Come see them march-ing all a-round,
ban - da di suon - a - tor', di suon - a - tor', di suon - a - tor',

O, Ca - te - ri - na, Ca - te - ri - na, my heart's a-pound; O, Ca - te - ri - na,
O, Ca - te-ri - na, Ca - te - ri-na, che bat - ti-cuor; O, Ca - te-ri - na,

Ca - te - ri - na, my heart's a-pound. The lead-er in
Ca - te - ri - na, che bat - ti - cuor. Il ca - po -

stride is burst-ing with pride, his but-tons of gold are a sight to see;
ban - da, il ca - po - ban - da, il ca - po - ban-da, i' bot - to - ni d'or,

He sets your heart a-fly-ing free,　O, Ca-te-ri-na, he's the love of your life,
sor - ri-de ogn' or', che ru-ba cuor,　O, Ca-te-ri-na, ca - po - ban-da il tuo gran-

I see,　O, Ca - te - ri - na, he's the love of your life, I see.
de a-mor,　O, Ca - te - ri - na, ca - po - ban-da il tuo gran-de a-mor.

They're march-ing　by, ta - ran-ta - ra,　so la so mi do re mi
Ec - co - li　qua son tut - ti　qua,　so la so mi do re mi

fa. The drum-mer twirls his great mus-tache, gives ev - 'ry beat a thun-d'rous
fa. E con i baffor-ri a pant - o - lon' giun-ge il tam-bur - o　co - rre un

crash.   He's here!   He's here!   Yes,   yes, he's real - ly here!
tuon.   *È lui!*   *è lui!*   *si,   si   è pro-prio lui!*

He's   the   most im - por - tant drum-mer of all   in   Em - po - li,
È il Tam-bur - o   prin - ci - pal' del-la ban - da   d'Em - po - li,

Lead - er   of five hun-dred and fif - ty play-ers march-ing free.   How my
Che   co - man-da cin - que-cen-to cin-quan-ta   pi - ffe - ri;   Che pas -

heart swells with pride when they play "boom boom," and they march to and fro play-ing
sion, che e - mo - zion quan - do   fa "bum bum," Guar-da   qua men-tra van-no che

"oom-pah-pah."   All the girls are shy when he comes by so grand to see,
fan "pa - pa."   Le   ra - gaz-ze nel   ve - der-lo di-ven-tan'   ti - mi-de,

play - ing   all   the same no mat - ter what the   tune may be.   "Love - ly
lui   con - fon-de Il Tro - va - tor con la Se - mi - ra - mi-de.   "Bel - la

girl, come march a - long;   I   am yours, come with me and march a - long."
fi - glia dell' a - mor',   Schia-vo son, schia - vo son, i   vez - zi tuoi."

Band Music from England

Many famous composers have written pieces for concert band. Here is a concert band piece to listen to. You will probably recognize one of the themes.

Suite for Band, "Fantasia on Dargason"..............Gustav Holst

Meet the Composer

Gustav Holst was an English composer whose music was often inspired by Asian subjects or English folklore. His best-known work is a piece for orchestra called *The Planets*. It is based on the seven planets in the solar system, aside from Earth, that were known in his time.

Holst was a very important teacher of music. He might have taught more during his career, but his health was poor and working at composing was often very difficult for him.

Holst's two band suites are among the best and most important works for concert band.

Gustav Holst   (1875–1935)

Swing Bands
in the
United States

Many schools have concert bands—perhaps your school has one, too! From the concert band, other kinds of ensembles are often formed. Many members participate in marching bands, the perfect musical background for parades and sports events. Band musicians can also form a stage band, using instruments from the swing era bands of the 1930s and 40s. Stage bands often perform jazz and rock pieces in addition to arrangements from the swing era.

Listen to these famous pieces written in the 1940s. Do you recognize the style of the music?

 A String of Pearls ....Jerry Gray

 In the Mood ....Glenn Miller

*B*ands from Many *C*ultures

When you hear the word *band*, you probably think of either brass bands or rock bands. However, bands can be made up of many different kinds of instruments and can serve many different functions. It just depends on where you are in the world!

Listen to these bands, or **ensembles**, from different regions of the world. Can you tell, both from the recordings and the photographs of the ensembles above, what kinds of instruments are being used?

 Qunapaquí (Why?) ....Traditional Ensemble from Bolivia

 Chunjiang huayueye (A Beautiful Moonlit Night on the River in Springtime) ....Traditional Ensemble from China

 Senegalese Drumming ....Traditional Ensemble from Senegal

Dance— A World Tradition

Throughout the ages, dancing has had a strong impact on the music of the time.

The Jolly Flatboatmen *George Caleb Bingham*

Private Collection, on loan to the National Gallery of Art, Washington, D.C.

Early cultures from every part of the world danced to chanting, clapping, and the sound of drums and other instruments.

In ancient Western civilizations, dance training was required as part of the standard education of the young people.

Dance means different things to different people. It can be part of an important celebration or religious ceremony. It can be performed for others as entertainment. It can serve as a social occasion for friends to get together. Or it can be a personal way of expressing one's feelings and emotions.

As you listen to the following dances from around the world, can you guess what the purpose or function of each dance might be?

 Kelo aba w'ye ....Traditional Dance from Ghana

 Troika ....Traditional Dance from Russia

 Samoan Coconut ....Traditional Dance from Polynesia

 **D**ance in the **J**ewish **T**radition

America has a rich cultural heritage, much of it borrowed from other countries. Our country has adopted the spirit, traditions, and dance patterns of a multitude of immigrants. "Hava Nagila" goes with a popular circle dance called the hora.

Listen to another Jewish dance. How is it similar to "Hava Nagila"?

 Mayim! Mayim! ....Traditional Jewish Dance

Hava Nagila

Jewish Folk Song

2.

v' - nis - m' - ka. U - ru, u - ru a - chim,
vuh - nis - muh-khah oo - roo oo - roo ah - kheem

u - ru a - chim b'-lev sa - me - ach, u - ru a - chim b'-lev sa - me - ach,
oo-roo ah-kheem buh-lev sah - may-ah'kh oo-roo ah-kheem buh-lev sah - may-ah'kh

u - ru a - chim b'-lev sa - me - ach, u - ru a - chim b'-lev sa - me - ach,
oo-roo ah-kheem buh-lev sah - may-ah'kh oo-roo ah-kheem buh-lev sah - may-ah'kh

u - ru a - chim, u - ru a - chim b'lev sa - me - ach.
oo-roo ah - kheem oo-roo ah - kheem b'lev sah - may - ah'kh

Square dancing originated in the United States during the mid-1800s. The steps are similar to those of a French dance called a *quadrille*, as well as other European ballroom dances of the time.

From Europe to America

Country Style

Words and Music by Johnny Burke and James Van Heusen

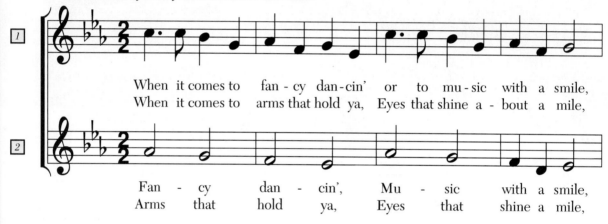

When it comes to fan-cy dan-cin' or to mu-sic with a smile,
When it comes to arms that hold ya, Eyes that shine a - bout a mile,

Fan - cy dan - cin', Mu - sic with a smile,
Arms that hold ya, Eyes that shine a mile,

Clap:

Or to nice ro - man - cin', Make mine coun - try style.
Like I just now told ya, Make mine coun - try style.

Clap:

Or to nice ro - man - cin', Make mine coun - try style.
Like I just now told ya, Make mine coun - try style.

Solo first time
All second time

Hear that fid - dle! I could lis - ten all night.

The energy and high spirits of the traditional square dance can be heard in this song, which was written for the movie *Welcome Stranger* in 1947.

All shout:

Hear that ban-jo! Ain't that some-thin'? All right!

1 Dance and share a lov-in' cup with dif-f'rent part-ners for a-while,

2 Dance with dif-f'rent part - ners for a-while,

Clap: D.S.

1 But for hitch-in' up with, Make mine coun-try style.

Clap:

2 But for hitch-in' up with, Make mine coun-try style.

Last time Shout: > >

1 Make mine coun-try style. _____ All right!

Last time Shout: > >

2 Make mine coun-try style. _____ All right!

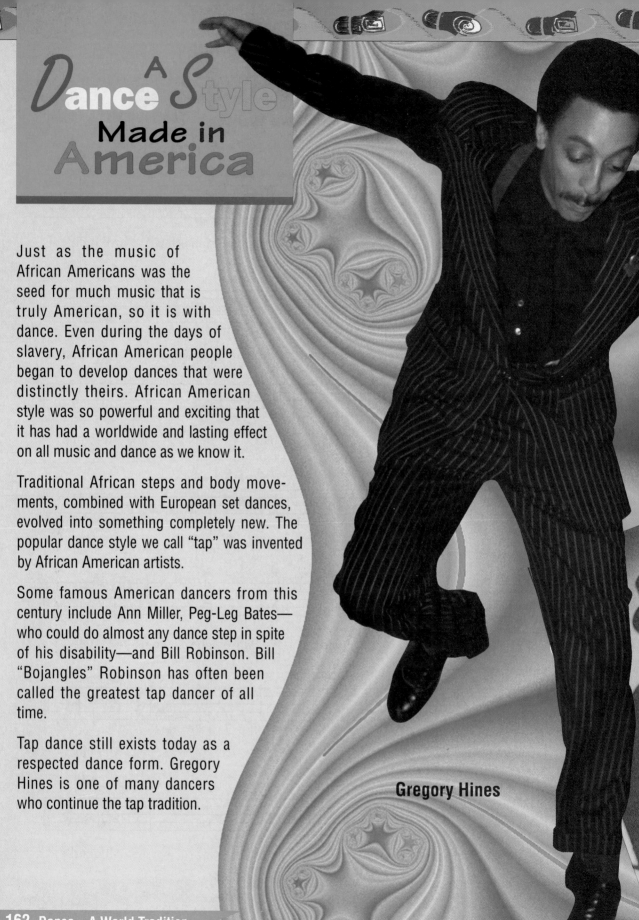

Dance ^A Style Made in America

Just as the music of African Americans was the seed for much music that is truly American, so it is with dance. Even during the days of slavery, African American people began to develop dances that were distinctly theirs. African American style was so powerful and exciting that it has had a worldwide and lasting effect on all music and dance as we know it.

Traditional African steps and body movements, combined with European set dances, evolved into something completely new. The popular dance style we call "tap" was invented by African American artists.

Some famous American dancers from this century include Ann Miller, Peg-Leg Bates—who could do almost any dance step in spite of his disability—and Bill Robinson. Bill "Bojangles" Robinson has often been called the greatest tap dancer of all time.

Tap dance still exists today as a respected dance form. Gregory Hines is one of many dancers who continue the tap tradition.

Gregory Hines

Ann Miller

Bill Robinson

Peg-Leg Bates

Dance Craze Days

During the twenty years between 1910 and 1930, Americans went dance crazy! Dance fads came and went with real twentieth-century speed.

There were dance songs—songs that gave instructions for steps and movements in the lyrics. There were also dance marathons, where couples danced continuously until exhaustion forced them to stop. Sometimes the marathons would last for several days.

The Charleston was probably the greatest dance craze of all.

Charleston

Words and Music by Cecil Mack and Jimmy Johnson

Charles-ton, _ Charles-ton, _ Made in ___ Car-o - li - na, ___

Some dance, _ some prance, _ I'll say _ There's noth-ing fin - er than the

Charles-ton, _ Charles-ton, _ Oh, how _ you can shuf - fle, _

Ev'ry step _ you do leads to some-thing new, Man, I'm tell - ing you

It's a la - pa-zoo! Buck dance, _ wing dance, _ will be ___ a back

num - ber, _ but the Charles-ton, _ the new Charles-ton, _ that dance _ is

sure-ly a com - er, Some-time ___ you'll _ dance it one time, _

The dance _ called the Charles-ton, ___ made in South _ Car-o - line. ___

A Ballet from Russia

Ballet is one of the most demanding and disciplined forms of dance. Ballet dancers have to be in terrific physical shape to endure the many hours of practicing and performing.

Let's take a look at one of Igor Stravinsky's most famous ballets, *Petrouchka*. The setting of the story is late nineteenth-century Russia. The excerpt you are about to hear is taken from the fair scene and features themes that represent four of the characters found at this winter celebration. The themes will serve as guides to your listening as well as ideas from which to create movement for each character.

 Petrouchka, Themes from Scene IV
................Igor Stravinsky

Play the following themes on mallet instruments. How would you finish them? Try inventing phrase endings.

Nursemaid's Theme

Try playing the Nursemaid and Bootman themes together as they appear in the ballet.

Bootman's Theme

What kind of movement would best express the legato feeling of the Nursemaid's theme and the marcato feeling of the Bootman's theme?

Walking a half note beat, can you invent a dance that struts—similar to the rich merchant passing through the crowds?

Merchant's Theme

Here is another theme to complete—the Groom's dance. Then listen to the recording to discover how Stravinsky completed his version.

Groom's Theme

This theme calls for similar dance motions. What kinds of steps will you take to copy this heaviness in movement? What qualities of movement will you use for your arms?

Song and Dance—
Musical Theater

The United States has given birth to a special kind of popular musical theater. It grew out of European opera and operetta traditions. Musical theater productions, or **musicals**, have gained enormous popularity over the past few decades. Today they are performed throughout the world in a variety of languages.

The Music Man, an all-American musical classic written by Meredith Willson in 1957, features the marching band dance-song "Seventy-Six Trombones." This song makes you want to be a part of the big parade!

 The Music Man, "Seventy-Six Trombones"............Meredith Willson

"Mr. Mistoffelees" is a most clever and magical cat from the musical *Cats*, by Andrew Lloyd Webber. He crouches, he stalks, he pounces—just listen to the song that describes his cunning ways!

 Cats, "Mr. Mistoffelees"
..............Andrew Lloyd Webber

The moment the music begins, you're ready to move into a step-dance routine. So, snap your fingers, throw back those shoulders, lift your head high, hold that top hat, and put on your best smile. Count *1 – 2 – 3 – 4 – 5 – 6 – 7 – 8 – "One!"* You are now a part of one of the greatest kick lines ever seen on the Broadway stage! The show is *A Chorus Line*, by Marvin Hamlisch.

 A Chorus Line, "One"
...........Marvin Hamlisch

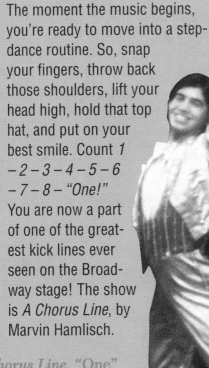

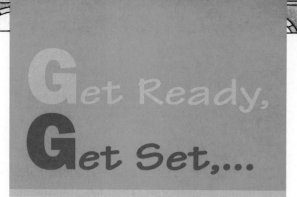

Get Ready, Get Set,...

Before you can speak or sing, you first have to breathe. The breath you take is very important when you are singing.

If you breathe correctly, you can expand your lungs to hold a greater volume of air. This will make it easier to sing. You can then sing longer without taking a breath, and you will have more air to help you control your singing.

When you are quietly breathing, the air is released through your mouth or nose with very little sound. When you want to sing or speak, you let the air vibrate a set of vocal cords, or folds deep in your throat. This is the way the sound is created.

The higher you want to sing or speak, the faster the cords must vibrate. You are so used to the way you change the pitch of your voice that you do not have to think about how you do it. It simply seems to happen.

However, you can control the sound, the pitch and loudness, even the tone quality of your voice. And you use your breath to control all of these changes.

Making Musical Phrases

Sing this song, taking a breath only at the end of each phrase line. Notice that some phrases are longer than others. You will need more breath for these longer phrases.

Bye-Bye, Blues

Words and Music by Fred Hamm, Dave Bennett, Bert Lown, and Chauncey Gray

Bye - bye, blues. ___ Bye - bye, blues. ___

Bells ring, birds sing, Sun is shin - ing. No more pin - ing.

Just we two ___ Smil - ing through. ___

Don't sigh, Don't cry, Bye - bye, blues. ___

Warming Up

If you go early to a sports event, you'll probably see players going through exercises that get their muscles ready for the game. Without these warm-up exercises, they will not play as well and they risk injuring muscles that are not prepared.

Musicians warm up their voices or instruments before beginning to make music. Here are some warm-up exercises.

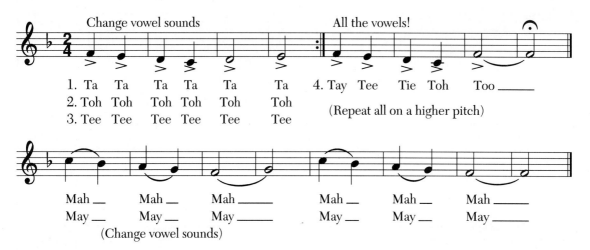

Change vowel sounds

All the vowels!

1. Ta   Ta   Ta   Ta   Ta   Ta   4. Tay Tee Tie Toh   Too _____
2. Toh Toh Toh Toh Toh Toh
3. Tee Tee Tee Tee Tee Tee   (Repeat all on a higher pitch)

Mah __   Mah __   Mah _____   Mah __   Mah __   Mah _____
May __   May __   May _____   May __   May __   May _____

(Change vowel sounds)

Once your voice is warmed up, try singing "Charlottetown."

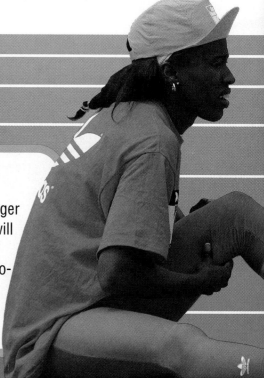

Singing with Style

Different songs need different voices. The tone quality a singer chooses for a song can completely change the style. How will you decide on the tone quality and style for a song? Where will you breathe? How do you think the words should be pronounced? Are there places where you would sing louder? Softer? In other words, how can you use your voice to interpret a song in the best possible way?

Here is a song that tells a story. There are three verses with a refrain in between each verse and at the end. As you sing, imagine that you are telling the story to an audience. Pronounce the words as clearly as possible so a listener can follow the story.

Dona Dona

Words and Music by Sholom Secunda   *English Words by Arthur Kevess and Teddi Schwartz*

Guitar: capo 5

1. On a wag - on bound for mar - ket   there's a calf with a
2. "Stop com - plain - ing," said the far - mer,   "Who told you a ___
3. Calves are eas - i - ly bound and slaught - ered,   nev - er know-ing the

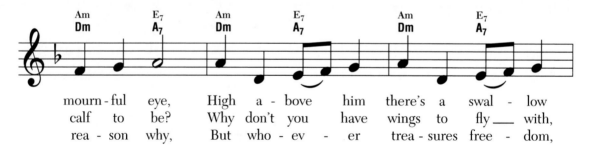

mourn - ful eye,   High a - bove him there's a swal - low
calf to be?   Why don't you have wings to fly ___ with,
rea - son why,   But who - ev - er trea - sures free - dom,

wing-ing swift - ly ___ through the sky.   How the winds are
like the swal - low so proud and free?"
like the swal - low has learned to fly.

As you perform "Dona Dona," you will find that the **accelerando** section at the end will be the most difficult part of the song. Accelerando means "to get faster and faster." You will have to listen carefully to your classmates to stay together.

laugh - ing, They laugh with all their might.

Laugh and laugh the whole day through, and half the sum-mer's night.

Accelerando

Do-na, do-na, do - na, do - na, Do-na, do-na, do - na, __ don,

Do-na, do-na, do - na, do - na, Do-na, do-na, do - na, don.

Do - na, do - na, do - na, don.

Singing

Whether you perform a song with movement, or just by standing and singing, there is one thing to remember—an audience is looking at you when you perform. You should have a pleasant face when you are singing.

Always look at the conductor. Try to show the feeling of the music on your face.

Sheep May Safely Graze

English Words by Linda Williams   *Music by J. S. Bach*

God, our _shep-herd, in   thy _keep-ing, _   safe _ in thy care, for

all our _ days, God, our _shep-herd, wak-ing, _sleep-ing, _ Lead and _ guide _ us, _

Walk be - side _ us, _ So thy sheep _ may _ safe - ly graze.   So _ thy _

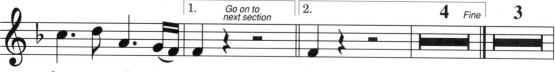

sheep may safe - ly _ graze.   graze.

Give us cour-age when we fal - ter; _ Ease the _ bur-dens we must _ bear. Let our

3

hearts re - joice in thy lov - ing _ care. Turn thy _

face to shine _ up-on us, _ when the _ storm - y wind _ and

rain de - scend, _ Be our _ shep - herd and friend, _ No _ harm _

poco rit. *D.S. al Fine*

_ shall come to us with _ thee watch-ing _ o - ver _ us _ till _ jour-ney's _ end.

Stage Movement

Sharing Music with an Audience

Performing music in front of an audience means sharing the music with people who are watching and listening. A good performance delivers a message to the audience, and that takes a lot of planning. You will have to decide how to stand or move to interpret the song.

If you want an audience to pay attention to you, you must pay attention to them. Remember, for an audience, the most important part of your face is your eyes!

Creating Movement

Some songs work well with movement. If you are singing in a group, it is very effective if everyone makes the same movements together. Coordinated movement is one of the best ways to make an audience pay attention.

You can also "underline" important words in a song with movements. Sometimes just bringing out a single word can be very effective. However, you should always make the movements natural and appropriate to the song. Crazy actions on the stage can be a lot of fun for both the performers and the audience, but even comical antics should be planned and well-rehearsed.

Creating Movement to Music

Aaron Copland wrote the ballet *Appalachian Spring* for famous dancer Martha Graham. In one of the most famous parts of the ballet, he wrote a set of variations based on the tune "Simple Gifts."

Consider how you might create a movement for each of the first four variations using a variety of movement qualities. The movement variations should begin with the music, one at a time, and melt to the floor at the conclusion of their part. All movements can then be combined for the final variation.

Appalachian Spring, "Variations on 'Simple Gifts'" ....Copland

Putting it All Together

How will you use your voice to deliver this song's message? What types of movement will you use to illustrate this song?

Eres tú   (Touch the Wind)

English words by Mike Hawker   *Words and Music by Juan Carlos Calderón*

Co-mo u-na pro-me-sa, ___ e-res tú, ___ e-res tú.
I woke up this morn-ing, ___ and my mind ___ fell a-way,

Co-mo u-na ma-ña-na, ___ de ve-ra-no.
Look-ing back sad-ly ___ from to-mor-row.

Co-mo u-na son-ri-sa, ___ e-res tú, ___ e-res tú, ___ A-sí, ___
As I heard an ech-o ___ from the past ___ soft-ly say ___ Come back, __

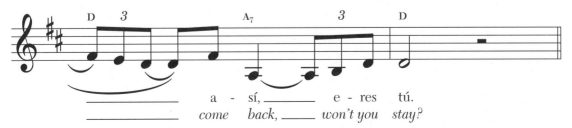

___ a-sí, ___ e-res tú.
___ come back, ___ won't you stay?

Careers in Music— Billy Joel

Very few popular musicians are able to remain popular for very long in today's changing musical environment. Billy Joel is one of the exceptions. His skills as a pianist, composer, and lyricist allow him to write music that is enjoyed by people all over the world.

In the first part of this recorded interview, Billy Joel describes the start of his musical career.

 Interview with Billy Joel—Part I

Listen as Billy describes his music and tells what it is like to be an entertainer to millions of people.

 Interview with Billy Joel—Part II

 The Ballad of Billy the Kid ....Billy Joel

 We Didn't Start the Fire ....Billy Joel

Careers in Music—
Tania León

Composer, conductor, performer, teacher—Tania León has a great deal of experience and talent in each of these roles. Listen as she describes her background and her sources of musical inspiration.

Interview with Tania León

Indigena............Tania León

Leaders for Freedom

What current-day leaders or heroes could you add to this song?

Abraham, Martin, and John

Words and Music by Dick Holler   *Arranged by Joan R. Hillsman*

Has an-y-bod-y here seen my old friend 1. A - bra-ham?
2. Mar - tin?
3. John? ___
4. Bob - by?

Can you tell me where he's gone? _____

1.-3. He freed a lot-ta peo - ple, but it seems the good die
4. I thought I saw him walk - in' up ___ o - ver the

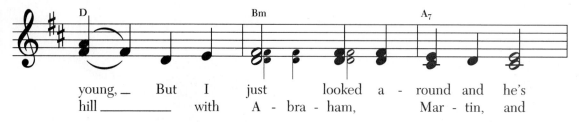

young, ___ But I just looked a - round and he's
hill _____ with A - bra - ham, Mar - tin, and

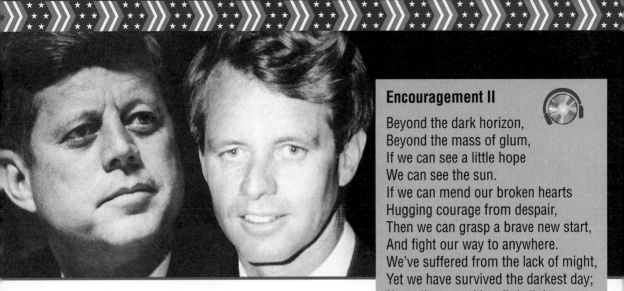

Encouragement II

Beyond the dark horizon,
Beyond the mass of glum,
If we can see a little hope
We can see the sun.
If we can mend our broken hearts
Hugging courage from despair,
Then we can grasp a brave new start,
And fight our way to anywhere.
We've suffered from the lack of might,
Yet we have survived the darkest day;
Now all we need is a little light
And we will find our way.

John Henrik Clarke

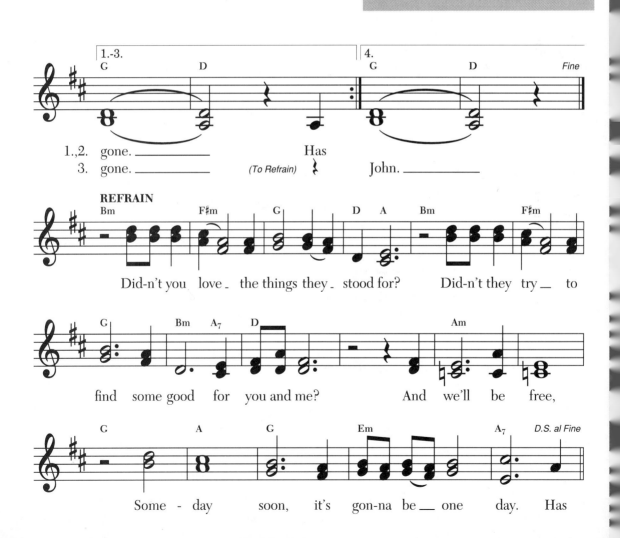

1.,2. gone. _____ Has
3. gone. _____ *(To Refrain)* John. _____

REFRAIN

Did-n't you love _ the things they _ stood for? Did-n't they try _ to

find some good for you and me? And we'll be free,

Some - day soon, it's gon-na be _ one day. Has

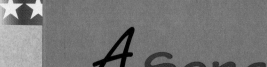

A Song for Freedom

Free at Last

African American Spiritual   *Arranged by Joan R. Hillsman*

Free at last, _ free at last, _ Thank God Al-might-y I'm free at last. _

Free at last, _ free at last, _____ Thank God Al-might-y I'm free at last. _

'Way down yon-der in the grave-yard walk,
On a my knees _ when the light pass'd by,
Some a these morn - ings, _ bright and fair,

Gon-na

Chorus

Thank God Al-might-y I'm free at last. _

Our National Anthem

Our national anthem is an expression of victory over enemies of freedom.

The Star-Spangled Banner

Words by Francis Scott Key   Music by John Stafford Smith

1. Oh, __ say! can you see, by the dawn's ear - ly light, What so
2. On the shore, dim - ly seen through the mists of the deep, Where the
3. Oh, __ thus be it ever when __ free men shall stand Be -

proud - ly we hailed at the twi - light's last gleam - ing, Whose broad
foe's haugh - ty host in dread si - lence re - pos - es, What is
tween their loved homes and the war's des - o - la - tion! Blest with

stripes and bright stars, through the per - il - ous fight, O'er the
that which the breeze, o'er the tow - er - ing steep, As it
vic - t'ry and peace, may the heav'n - res - cued land Praise the

ram - parts we watched were so gal - lant - ly stream - ing? And the
fit - ful - ly blows, half con - ceals, half dis - clos - es? Now it
Pow'r that hath made and pre - served us a na - tion! Then __

rock - ets' red glare, the bombs burst - ing in air, Gave
catch - es the gleam of the morn - ing's first beam, In full
con - quer we must, for our cause it is just, And

proof through the night that our flag was still there. Oh,
glo - ry re - flected now _ shines on the stream; 'Tis the
this be our motto: "In _ God is our trust!" And the

say, does that _ Star-Span-gled Ban - ner _ yet _ wave _ O'er the
Star-Span - gled _ Ban - ner, oh, long may _ it _ wave _ O'er the
Star-Span - gled _ Ban - ner in tri - umph _ shall _ wave _ O'er the

land _____ of the free and the home of the brave?
land _____ of the free and the home of the brave!
land _____ of the free and the home of the brave!

From Sea to Shining Sea

America, the Beautiful

Words by Katharine Lee Bates   *Music by S. A. Ward*

1. O beau - ti - ful for spa - cious skies, For am - ber waves of grain,
2. O beau - ti - ful for pil - grim feet, Whose stern im - pas - sioned stress
3. O beau - ti - ful for pa - triot dream That sees be - yond the years

For pur - ple moun - tain maj - es - ties A - bove the fruit - ed plain!
A thor - ough - fare for free - dom beat A - cross the wil - der - ness!
Thine al - a - bas - ter cit - ies gleam, Un - dimmed by hu - man tears!

A - mer - i - ca! A - mer - i - ca! God shed His grace on thee
A - mer - i - ca! A - mer - i - ca! God mend thine ev - 'ry flaw,
A - mer - i - ca! A - mer - i - ca! God shed His grace on thee

And crown thy good with broth - er - hood From sea to shin - ing sea!
Con - firm thy soul in self - con - trol, Thy li - ber - ty in law!
And crown thy good with broth - er - hood From sea to shin - ing sea!

 America, the Beautiful (gospel version) ....Bates/Ward

Let Freedom Ring

America

Words by Samuel Francis Smith   *Traditional Melody*

1. My coun-try! 'tis of thee, Sweet land of lib-er-ty,
2. My na-tive coun-try, thee, Land of the no-ble free,
3. Let mu-sic swell the breeze, And ring from all the trees
4. Our fa-ther's God, to Thee, Au-thor of li-ber-ty,

Of thee I sing; Land where my fa-thers died, Land of the
Thy name I love; I love thy rocks and rills, Thy woods and
Sweet free-dom's song; Let mor-tal tongues a-wake, Let all that
To Thee we sing; Long may our land be bright With Free-dom's

Pil-grims' pride, From ev-'ry moun-tain-side Let free-dom ring!
tem-pled hills; My heart with rap-ture thrills Like that a-bove.
breathe par-take, Let rocks their si-lence break, The sound pro-long.
ho-ly light, Pro-tect us by Thy might, Great God, our King!

This is a song to sing anytime, but you might want to save it for a special occasion!

I Am But a Small Voice

Original Words by Odina E. Batnag   *English Words and Music by Roger Whittaker*

I am but a   small voice,   I have but a   small dream: The
small voice,   I have but a   small dream: To

frag-rance of a flower   in the un-pol-lut-ed air.   I am but a
smile up - on the sun,   be ___

free to dance _ and sing,   Be free to sing _ my song ev-'ry-where.

Come, young cit - i-zens of the world;   We are   one,   we are

one.   one. _____   We have one hope,

we have one dream,   and with one voice   we sing.

rit. *last time*

Fine

Countermelody

1 Give us peace, _ pros-per-i-ty, __ And love for all man-kind.

Melody

2 Peace, pros-per-i-ty, __ And love for all man - kind.

3 I am but a small voice, _ I have but a small _ dream: _ To smile up-on the

D.S. al Fine

sun, Be free to dance _ and sing, Be free to sing _ my song to ev-'ry-one.

Barter

Life has loveliness to sell,
All beautiful and splendid things,
Blue waves whitened on a cliff,
Soaring fire that sways and sings,
And children's faces looking up
Holding wonder like a cup.

Life has loveliness to sell,
Music like a curve of gold,
Scent of pine trees in the rain,
Eyes that love you, arms that hold,
And for your spirit's still delight,
Holy thoughts that star the night.

Spend all you have for loveliness,
Buy it and never count the cost;
For one white singing hour of peace
Count many a year of strife well lost,
And for a breath of ecstasy
Give all you have been, or could be.

Sara Teasdale

Harvest Time

Harvest time in the fall is traditionally a time of feasting and celebrating in many countries. In America, we mark the passing of the growing season with the feast of Thanksgiving.

Thanksgiving   *Mattie Lou O'Kelly*

From *Mattie Lou O'Kelley: Folk Artist.* © 1989 by Mattie Lou O'Kelley. By permission of Little, Brown & Co.

Come, Ye Thankful People, Come

Words by Henry Alford   Music by George J. Elvey

1. Come, ye thank-ful   peo - ple, come,   Raise the song of   har-vest home;
2. All   the bless-ings   of the field,   All   the stores the   gar-dens yield;

All   is safe - ly   gath - ered in,   Ere the win - ter   storms be - gin;
All   the fruits in   full sup-ply,   Rip-ened 'neath the   sum - mer sky;

God, our Mak - er,   doth pro - vide   For our wants to   be sup-plied;
All   that spring with   boun-teous hand   Scat - ters o'er the   smil-ing land;

Come to God's own   tem - ple, come,   Raise the song of   har - vest home.
All   that lib - 'ral   au - tumn pours   From her rich o'er - flow-ing stores.

The celebration of Chanukah, the Jewish Festival of Lights, takes place on late fall dates that vary from year to year.

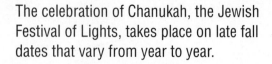

of Lights

O Chanukah

English Words by Judith Eisenstein *Jewish Folk Song*

O Cha-nu-kah, O Cha-nu-kah, come light the me-no-rah.
Let's __ have a par - ty, we'll all dance the ho - rah.

Gath-er round the ta - ble, we'll give you a treat,

Shin-ing tops to play with and pan - cakes to eat;

And while we are play-ing, The can-dles are burn-ing __ low,

One for each night, they __ shed a sweet light to re -

mind us of days long a - go,   mind us of days long a - go.

From GATEWAYS TO JEWISH SONG, collected and translated by Judith Eisenstein. Used by permission.

A favorite part of the holiday is the lighting of the candles of the menorah, one candle on each of the eight nights of Chanukah.

Lighting the Menorah

Around About Chanukah

Words and Music by David Eddleman

Chan-u - kah comes but once a year with sto-ries of an-cient days.

Tell-ing a won-drous tale of how the lan-tern re-mained a - blaze.

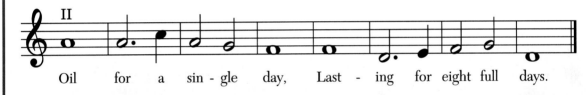

Oil for a sin - gle day, Last - ing for eight full days.

Accompany this round with a rhythm pattern on the tambourine.

(repeat)

Bells, Recorder, Keyboard

A Classical Holiday Round

Gloria, Gloria

Music by Franz Joseph Haydn

Glo - ri - a,   Glo - ri - a   in ex - cel - sis,   Glo - ri - a.

Glo - ri - a,   Glo - ri - a   in ex - cel - sis,   Glo - ri - a.

Glo - ri - a,   Glo - ri - a   in ex - cel - sis,   Glo - ri - a.

Et   in   ter - ra   pax ____ ho - min - i - bus.

Et ____ in   ter - ra   pax ____ ho - min - i - bus.

Et ____ in   ter - ra   pax   ho - min - i - bus.

Silent Night

Words by Joseph Mohr   Music by Franz Gruber

Guitar: capo 3

Si - lent night,   ho - ly night,   All   is   calm,
Stil - le Nacht,   Hei - li - ge Nacht,   Al - les schläft,
No - che de   paz,   no - che de a - mor,   To - do duerme en

all   is bright   Round yon Vir - gin Moth - er and Child.
ein - sam wacht   Nur   das trau - te hoch - hei - li - ge Paar.
de - rre - dor.   Entre los as - tros que es - par - cen su   luz,

Ho - ly In - fant so   ten - der and mild,   Sleep   in heav - en - ly
Hol - der Kna - be im   lok - ki - gen Haar,   Schlaf' in himm - lisch - er
Bella a - nun - cian - do al ni - ñi - to Je - sús,   Brilla la es - tre - lla de

peace, ____   Sleep __ in heav - en - ly   peace. ____
Ruh, _____   Schlaf' __ in himm - lisch - er   Ruh. _____
paz, _____   Bri - lla la es - tre - lla de   paz. _____

This carol has a countermelody for the higher voices.

Ding-Dong Merrily On High

English Words by G. R. Woodward   Carol from France

3. Ding-dong   mer - ri - ly,   in heav'n   the

1., 3. Ding-dong! mer - ri - ly on high   in heav'n the bells are
2. Pray you, du - ti - ful - ly prime   your mat - in chime, ye

bells _ are _ ring - ing.   Ding-dong   ver - i - ly,   on

ring   -   ing.   Ding-dong! ver - i - ly the sky   is
ring   -   ers.   May you beau-ti - ful - ly rime   your

high   the   an - gel _ sing - ing.   Glo   -   ri -

riv'n with an - gel sing   -   ing.   Glo   -   -   -
eve - time song, ye sing   -   ers.

a, Glo‑ri‑a Glo‑ri‑a, Ho‑ — — — — — — — — — — —

san‑na, ho‑san‑na in ex‑cel‑sis!

— — — ‑ri‑a, Ho‑san‑na in ex‑cel‑sis!

Angel Playing Violin *Melozzo da Forli*

Angel Playing the Lute *Melozzo da Forli*

A **Two-Part Song to Share**

Christmas Is a Time for Sharing

Words and Music by David Eddleman

Christ-mas time is a time for shar - ing, Christ-mas time is a time for car-

- ing, A time for ev-'ry-one _ to cel - e - brate and sing a hap-py

song. Christ-mas time is a time for giv - ing, It's a time for some hap-py liv-

- ing, It's a time when ev-'ry-one can car-ol Christ-mas loud and long. _

1 Christ-mas time is a time for sing - ing, Christ-mas

2 Christ - mas time is
    Christ - mas time is

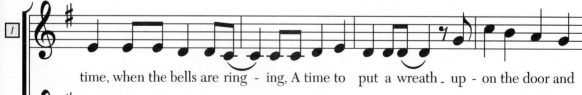

1 time, when the bells are ring - ing, A time to put a wreath _ up - on the door and

2

lov - ing time, a time for ev - 'ry -
sing - ing time, a time for tin - sel

An Old English Christmas

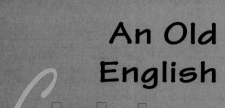

This beautiful carol has been a favorite for many centuries.

The Holly and the Ivy

Traditional Carol from England   *Arranged by Mary Hoffman*

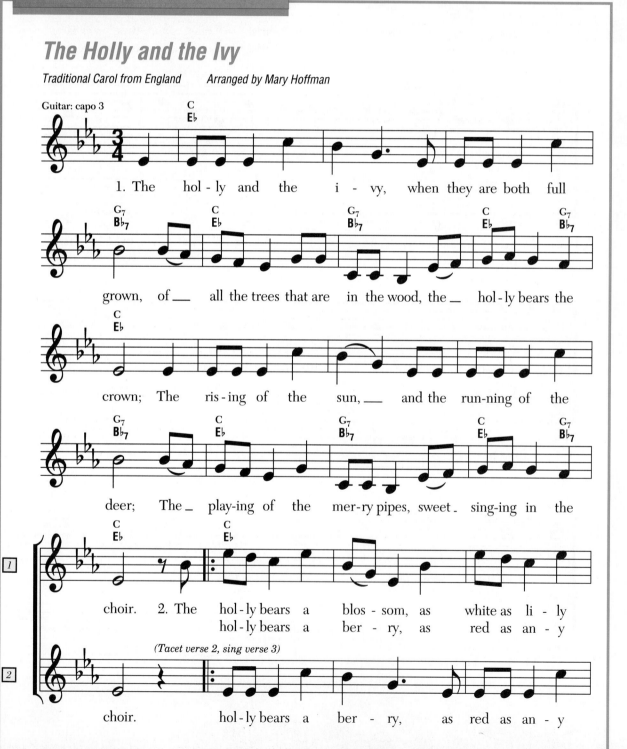

1. The hol-ly and the i-vy, when they are both full grown, of ___ all the trees that are in the wood, the ___ hol-ly bears the crown; The ris-ing of the sun, ___ and the run-ning of the deer; The ___ play-ing of the mer-ry pipes, sweet ___ sing-ing in the choir. 2. The hol-ly bears a blos-som, as white as li-ly hol-ly bears a ber-ry, as red as an-y choir.

(Tacet verse 2, sing verse 3)

hol-ly bears a ber-ry, as red as an-y choir.

Winter Wonderland
Word Play

Our senses respond in a variety of ways to the exploration of a winter wonderland. We *feel* the cold, *taste* the bite of the wind, *smell* the frosty air, *see* the sun shimmering off icicles and frozen ponds, and *hear* the crunch of snow beneath our feet. These reactions can be translated into word pictures. Word pictures capture, with the imagination, what a photographer captures with a camera.

As you look at the following photographs of winter scenes, see if you can translate them into word pictures, creating winter-wonderland poetry. Then choose songs or listening selections from your book that you feel describe each photograph using the language of music. Listen first to *Winter Wonderland*. Which photograph best represents the mood of the song?

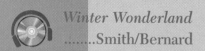

Winter Wonderland
........Smith/Bernard

The mountain was covered with snow, looking like. . .

Icicles dangle like ornaments off trees, feeling as wet as. . .

Snowflakes light up the air like laughter, looking like. . .

The snow has covered the roofs and trees as soundlessly as. . .

Who are the three characters that sing in this
Christmas ballad?

Good King Wenceslas

Traditional

1. Good King Wen-ces-las looked out   On the Feast of   Ste-phen,
2. "Hith-er, page, and stand by   me,   If thou know'st it,   tell-ing,
3. "Bring me flesh and bring me   wine, Bring me pine-logs hith-er,
4. "Sire, the night is   dark-er   now,   And the wind blows strong-er;
5. In his mas-ter's steps he   trod, Where the snow lay dint-ed;

When the snow lay   round a-bout,   Deep and crisp and   e-ven;
Yon-der pea-sant, who is   he?   Where and what his   dwell-ing?"
Thou and I will   see him dine, When we bear them thi-ther."
Fails my heart, I   know not how,   I can go no long-er."
Heat was in the   ver-y sod   Which the saint had print-ed.

Bright-ly shone the moon that night, Though the frost was   cru-el,
"Sire, he lives a   good league hence, Un-der-neath the moun-tain;
Page and mon-arch forth they   went, Forth they went to-geth-er;
"Mark my foot-steps, good my   page! Tread thou in them bold-ly;
There-fore, Chris-tian folk, be   sure, Wealth or rank pos-sess-ing;

When   a poor man came in sight, Gath-'ring win-ter fu-el.
Right   a-gainst the for-est fence, By Saint Ag-nes' foun-tain."
Through the rude wind's wild la-ment, And the bit-ter wea-ther.
Thou shalt find the   win-ter's rage Freeze thy blood less cold-ly."
Ye   who now will bless the poor, Shall your-selves find bless-ing.

Here is a contemporary version of the same carol performed by Mannheim Steamroller.

Good King Wenceslas .... Traditional Carol

We Wish You a Merry Christmas

Holiday Cheer!

Carol from England

1. We wish you a mer-ry Christ-mas, We wish you a mer-ry Christ-mas,
2. Now bring us some fig-gy pud-ding, Now bring us some fig-gy pud-ding,

We wish you a mer-ry Christ-mas, And a hap-py New Year!
Now bring us some fig-gy pud-ding, And bring it out here.

3. We won't go until we get some, . . .
   So bring some out here.

4. We wish you a merry Christmas, . . .
   And a happy New Year!

Bells or Keyboard

Countermelody

2. Now bring us some fig-gy pud-ding, Some
4. We wish you a mer-ry Christ-mas, A

fig-gy pud-ding, And bring it out here.
mer-ry Christ-mas and a hap-py New Year.

Cinco de Mayo!

In Mexico, Cinco de Mayo (the fifth of May) marks the 1862 victory of the Mexican army over French invaders. "Así es mi tierra" reflects the patriotic, celebratory spirit of the holiday.

Así es mi tierra

Words and Music by Ignacío Fernandez Esperón

A - sí es mi tie - rra, mo - re - ni - ta y lu - mi - no - sa;
ah-see ehs mee tee eh - rah moh-reh - nee-tah ee loo - mee - noh-sah

a - sí es mi tie - rra, tie - ne el al - ma he - cha de a - mor.
ah - see ehs mee tee eh-rah tee - nehl ahl-mah eh-chah deh ah - mohr

A - sí es mi tie - rra, a - bun - dán - te y ge - ne - ro - sa;
ah-see ehs mee tee eh-rah ah - boon-dahn - teh heh - neh - roh - sah

¡Ay, tie - rra mí - a co - mo es gra - to tu ca - lor!
ah ee tee eh-rah mee - ah koh-moh ehs grah - toh too kah - lohr

© Ignacío Fernandez Esperón.

Sus al-bo-ra-das tan lle-ni-tas, de a-le-grí-a.
soos ahl-boh-rah-thas tahn yeh-nee-tahs deh ah-leh-gree-ah

Sus se-re-na-tas tan pro-pi-cias al a-mor.
soos seh-reh-nah-tahs tahn proh-pee-cee ahs ahl ah-mohr

A-sí es mi tie-rra, flor de la me-lan-co-lí-a.
ah-see ehs mee tee eh-rah flohr deh lah meh-lahn-kah-lee-ah

¡Ay, tie-rra mí-a co-mo es gra-to tu ca-lor!
ah ee tee eh-rah mee-ah koh-moh ehs grah-toh too kah-lohr

A Multicultural Language

Love in Any Language

Words and Music by Jon Mohr and John Mays

Guitar: capo 1

Je t'aime. Te a - mo. Ya tri-bya lyu-blyu.
(French) *(Spanish)* *(Russian)*

A - ni o - he - vet-ot - ka. I love you. The
(Hebrew)

sounds are all as dif - f'rent as the lands from which they came. And

though our words are all u - nique, our hearts are still the same.

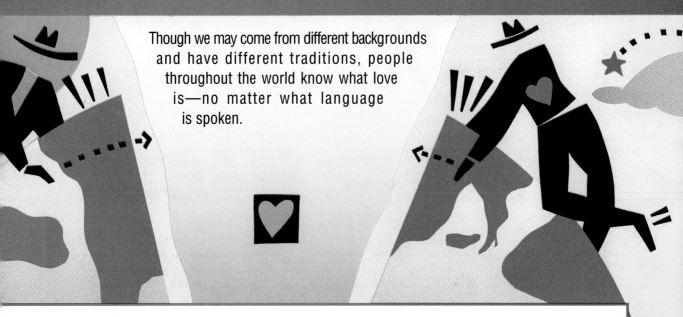

Though we may come from different backgrounds and have different traditions, people throughout the world know what love is—no matter what language is spoken.

REFRAIN

Love in an - y lan - guage, ___ straight from the heart, ___ Pulls us all ___ to - geth - er, ___ nev - er a - part. ___ And once we learn ___ to speak ___ it, ___ all the world ___ will hear, ___ Love in an - y lan - guage ___ flu - ent - ly spo - ken ___ here. We teach the young ___ our dif - f'renc - es, yet look how we're the same. _

2nd time to ⊕

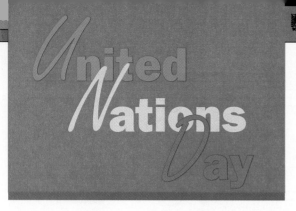

After World War II, countries throughout the world that had opposed the Axis powers decided that such a war should never happen again. Nations began to work together to find a solution. On October 24, 1945, the United Nations was formed to promote world peace and preserve human dignity. Today over 175 countries are members of this worldwide organization.

Sing a Song of Peace

Words and Arrangement by Jill Gallina   *"This Is My Country"–Words by Don Raye*   *Music by Al Jacobs*

1. Sing a song of peace through the world, till ev'ry land is sing-ing. —
2. This is my coun-try, land of my birth;

1. Sound the bells of peace through the world, with ev'ry na-tion ring-ing. —
2. This is my coun-try, grand - est on earth.

Land by land   'cross moun-tain and plain,   Hand in hand one long, lov-ing chain;

I   pledge thee my al - le   -   giance, A - mer-i-ca, _____ the bold.

rit. last time

Un - til peace and   free - dom _ reign   from sea _ to _ shin - ing

This   is   my   coun-try   to   have   and to

1.,2.   **3.**   ***pp***

sea.   sea.   Sing a song of peace.

pp

hold!   hold!   Sing a song of peace.

"Siyahamba" is a Zulu freedom song from South Africa. It is intended to be danced to. Listen for the syncopation in the music as the lyrics repeat again and again, *We are walking in the light of God.*

Siyahamba

Traditional Freedom Song from South Africa   *English Words and Arrangement by Rick Baitz*

Si-ya-ham-ba ___ Si-ya-ham-ba ___ Si-ya-

Si-ya-ham-ba Si-ya-ham-ba ___ Si-ya-ham-ba ___

ham-ba ___ Si-ya-ham-ba ___ Si-ya

Si-ya-ham-ba ___ Si-ya-ham-ba ___

ham-ba ___ Si-ya-ham-ba

Si-ya-ham-ba Si-ya-ham-ba

In 1985 a group of artists, including Sergio Mendes, Vikki Carr, Placido Domingo, Julio Iglesias, Miami Sound Machine, and José Feliciano, banded together to pledge their help to children of Latin America, the Caribbean, and Africa. Their foundation, *Hermanos* ("Brothers and Sisters"), has pledged that all proceeds from the sale of recordings of "Cantaré, cantarás" will be used for supplies of food and medicine to those most in need. The deeply moving lyrics express the love and hope of people helping people.

Cantaré, cantarás   *(I Will Sing, You Will Sing)*

English Words by Eileen Mahood-José
Arranged by Richard Kaller

Words and Music by Albert Hammond and Juan Carlos Calderón

Te da - ré ___ cuan - to pue - do dar, ___
I will give ___ all that I can give, ___

Só - lo sé can-tar ___ y pa - ra tí es mi can - to ___
I can on - ly sing, ___ and this song is my gift. _____

___ Y mi voz ___ Jun - to a los de - más, ___
___ And my voice ___ togeth-er with the rest, ___

En la in-men - si - dad ___ se es - tá ___ es - cu - chan - do.
ech - oes through the world ___ un - til ___ it ___ finds ___ suc-cess.

REFRAIN

Can - ta - ré _____ can - ta - rás _____
Ca - da vez _____ so - mos más _____
I will sing, _____ you will sing, _____
If you hold _____ out a hand, _____

Y e - sa luz _____ al fi - nal _____ del sen - de - ro.
Y si al fin _____ nos da - mos la ma - no
And a song _____ will bring ___ us to - geth - er.
And you nev - er let go _____ of your dream, _____

Bri - lla - rá _____ co - mo un sol _____ Que i - lu - mi -
Siem - pre ha - brá _____ un lu - gar _____ Pa - ra to -
And our hopes ___ and our prayers, __ We will make __
We'll make sure ___ there's a place ___ For __ ev -

1.   **2.** *(Last time repeat refrain ad lib)*

- na el mun - do en - te - ro.
- do ser _____ hu - ma - no.
__ them __ last ___ for - ev - er.
- ery hu - man __ be - ing.

Now listen to the original recording as performed by the *Hermanos* artists.

Cantaré, cantarás ....Hammond/Calderón

Russian composer Dmitri Shostakovich wrote the melody to this song, to which an American teacher later added lyrics. Shostakovich once said, "Music is no longer an end in itself, but a vital weapon in the struggle."

The United Nations *Raoul Dufy*

The United Nations

Words by Harold Rome   Music by Dmitri Shostakovich

Guitar:

1. The sun and the stars all are ring - ing, ___ With song ris-ing
2. Take heart all you na - tions swept un - der, ___ With pow - ers of
3. As sure as the sun meets the morn - ing, ___ And riv - ers go

from the __ earth. ___ The hope of hu - man - i - ty
dark - ness that ride, ___ The wrath of the peo - ple shall
down to the sea, ___ A new day for all is ___

sing - ing, ___ A hymn to a new world in birth.
thun - der, ___ Re - lent - less as time and the tide.
dawn - ing, ___ Our chil - dren shall live proud and free!

REFRAIN

U - ni - ted Na - tions on the march with

flags un - furl'd, ___ To - geth - er fight for

|1.| |2.|

vic - to - ry, a free New World. ___ To - World.

Introducing...

Ever have one of those days when everything seems to be going the wrong way? One of those days when everyone seems to be against you? One of those days when no one seems to understand you? Well, if you think you have it bad, you should meet Arnie...

IT'S A FAM'LY!

By
Ned Ginsburg and Cornelia Ravenal

Prologue
from "It's a Fam'ly"

Words by Cornelia Ravenal   *Music by Ned Ginsburg*

It's a fam - 'ly, _____ here is a fam - 'ly. _____ Some-one

in it does-n't know that or he does-n't care to show that he be - longs! _____

This is Ar - nie, _____ comf'r-ta-ble Ar - nie. _____

And though things may seem al-right, there is some-thing clear - ly...

I Need Help!

Words by Cornelia Ravenal   Music by Ned Ginsburg

Adult 1 Why is it when we're all work-ing you sit watch-ing T V like a lump?
Bro I don't get this mul-ti-pli-ca-tion biz.

I don't think you'd ev-en mind if you were watch-ing T V in a dump!
And Teach - er ___ says ___ to - mor - row ___ there's a quiz.

Ar - nie, what am I to do? Should I cov - er up the screen?
So, what's five ___ times ___ three and ___ four times five?

Is this ev - er gon - na end? You're prac - ti - c'ly thir-teen!
I'll ne - ver make it out - ta this test a - live!

Why should I keep talk-ing when I on - ly end up feel-ing like a chump?
You ___ said ___ that ___ with ___ num - bers you're a wiz.

Dialogue

I need help!   I need   loads ___ of
I need help!   I need   ma - jor

drool. *Dialogue* I need help! I need ser - ious help! An

ac-tress can-not help __ but need a line. I need help! I need some - one's

help! __ But may-be you can't stand that I might shine. *Dialogue*

Arnie
Why am I the one they nag? It's like a to-tal drag! "No

ifs, no ands, no buts!" Look, they're gon-na have a

cow. They do need help and now, *(Spoken:)* 'cause they're nuts! *Dialogue*

Adult 1
Why is it when we're all work-ing you sit watch-ing T V like a lump?

Bro
I don't get this mul - ti - pli-ca - tion biz.

Sis

Can't be -

help!   We need   big - time help!   A   fam-'ly on-ly func-tions as a

team.   We need help!   We need   Ar - nie's   help! _____

Bro / Sis   *Adult 1*

If   you don't lend   a   hand, _ we'll have   to... If   you don't pitch in   now, _

Adult 1 / Bro / Sis

I   might just... If   you   don't   shape up   soon, _ we're   going   to...

(Adult 2 cuts cable)   **6**

Arnie "No!"   *Adult 1:* "Isn't that extreme?"

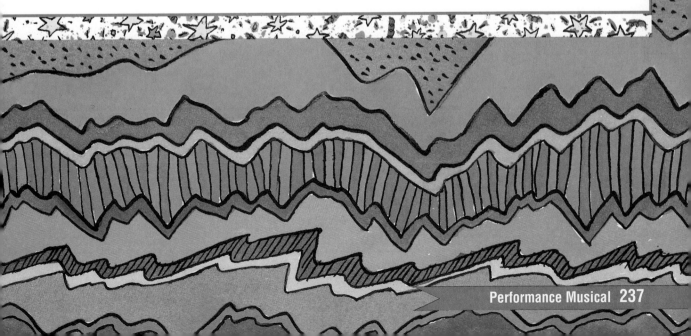

My Life

Words by Cornelia Ravenal   Music by Ned Ginsburg

Arnie

1. They tell me, "Kid, you know the rules," _ but rules just don't ap-ply to me.
2. Some peo-ple say a house di-vi - ded can-not stand in har-mo-ny.

(2nd time only)

They tell me, "Guy, don't snub your fam - 'ly," but
And then they say no man is an is - land.

Backup singers
(2nd time only)

Can-not stand in har-mo-ny.

they just give me mis-er - y.   If they don't
What's that got to do with me?   When will they

(2nd time only)

What's that got to do with me?

Pass the Ball

Words by Cornelia Ravenal   *Music by Ned Ginsburg*

In a "swung" rhythm

A-N-Y-T-O-W - N,   An-y-town's gon-na score a-gain! _

The   time is   now and the game is hot.   We got   twen-ty four sec-onds to make the shot.

Ar-nie, you know the win-ning play, _   so   start your stuff   and don't de-lay! _

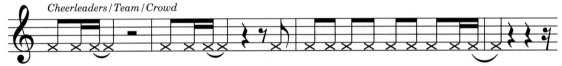

Pass the ball. _   Pass the ball. _   You're hard-ly ten feet tall, so pass the ball! _

We got six-teen sec-onds to ace the game, _ and Ar-nie thinks he's head-in' for the Hall of Fame. _

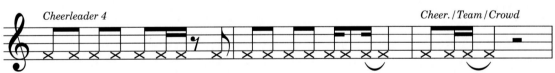

Don't be fool-ish, Mis-ter Big. You're act-ing like a   lit-tle pig! _   Pass the ball. _

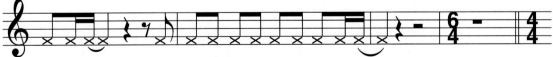

Pass the ball! _   This   ain't no time to stall, so pass the ball! _

Straight rhythm

Arnie

This is my chance to show my stuff. This is my chance to shine.

Pass-in' the ball is not e-nough.

Swung rhythm

But if I

drib-ble like cra-zy, fake to the cor - ner and take a three-point-

- er then all the glo-ry will be mine, on-ly mine!

Cheerleaders / Team / Crowd

Pass the ball! _ Pass the ball! _ You're look-in' aw-f'ly small, so pass the ball! _

There's a Boy I Dream Of

Words by Cornelia Ravenal   Music by Ned Ginsburg

Alice

There's a boy I dream of, and he's not like the boys I know. Though my

friends don't a-gree, what mat-ters to me is not the things that show.

There's a boy I dream of. No, he is-n't the per-fect boy. We will

have a good time, 'cause he'll know that I'm not some-bo-dy's toy. Who

cares if he's shy? Or if he can't dance? Who

cares if he's young? Or he's new to ro-mance? He won't

have to be smart _____ or a cap-tain of teams. _____ Won't

have to be cool. _____ Cool's not all that it seems. _

There's a boy I dream of, and I know if my dream comes true, _

I won't have to tell him, he'll know what I'll want him to do.

Arnie

There's a girl I dream of, and I know that she dreams of me. _ I'm the

kind of a guy _ who won't have to try to be what she wants me to be. _

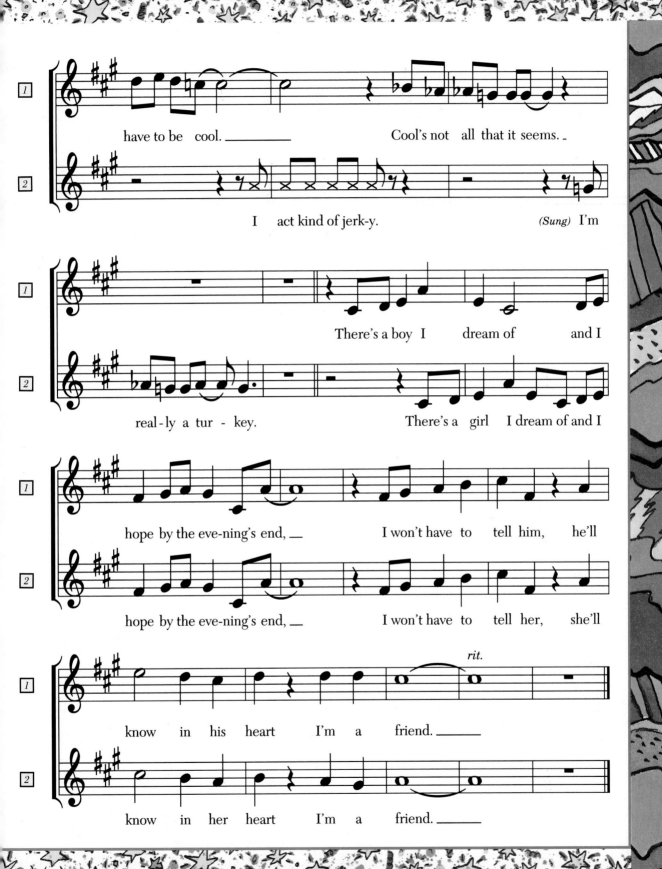

It's a Fam'ly

Words by Cornelia Ravenal   Music by Ned Ginsburg

A   nu-cle-us... that's a core.   Of in-di - vi-du-als...   that's

more.   It could be   an-y-thing...   like ants?   It could be   an-y-where...   like

France?   Liv-ing and work-ing...   like bea-vers?   All to - geth-er...   like the

Clea-vers? With sports there's a team, with mu-sic there's a band, but teams and bands don't

live to - geth-er. ____   Teams and bands on-ly work   to-geth-er! ____

Live and work,   work and live.   Come on, brain,   Some-thing's got-ta give!

(2nd time: key of D♭)
(3rd time: key of D)

It's a fam - 'ly! What is a fam - 'ly? That's the
fam - 'ly. We are a fam - 'ly. Here I
Part I fam - 'ly. We are a fam - 'ly. Here we

ques-tion to the an-swer to the ques-tion I should an-swer if I'm smart.
am be-long-ing to it and what's fun - ny is I knew it all a - long!
are be-long-ing to it and what's fun - ny is we knew it all a - long!

1

It's a fam-'ly! What is a fam - 'ly? That's the ques-tion to the
It's a fam-'ly. We are a fam - 'ly. Though we fight we're still to -
It's a fam-'ly. We are a fam - 'ly. Though we fight we're still to -

2

(2nd time) Family
(3rd time) Part II   It's a fam-'ly. We are a fam - 'ly. Though we fight we're still to -

It's a fam - 'ly. We are a fam - 'ly. _____ And in

It's a fam - 'ly. We are a fam-'ly. And in

all that we en-deav-or we'll be fam-i-ly for-ev-er and we'll al - ways work

all that we en-deav-or we'll be fam-i-ly for-ev-er and we'll al - ways work

as one. _____ *Part I* It's a al-ways work as one! _____

as one. _____ al-ways work as one! _____

READING

How do we know what music sounded like
hundreds of years ago?

How can musicians in the United States play music
that was written in Japan, Bolivia, or Senegal?

How do composers share their ideas
with other musicians?

Music notation is the key to answering these
questions. Music is a language—you need to know
how to speak it to understand and communicate
musical ideas with others. This section will
reinforce and expand the music reading abilities
you already have.

section 3

Can you tell if this is *do* pentatonic or *la* pentatonic?

A Pentatonic Song

Leatherwing Bat

Traditional

1. "Hi," said the lit - tle lea - ther - wing bat, "I'll tell you the rea - son that,

The rea - son that I fly by night Is be - cause I lost my heart's de - light."

REFRAIN

How - dy, dow - dy did - dle - o - day, How - dy, dow - dy did - dle - o - day,

How - dy, dow - dy did - dle - o - day, How - dy, dow - dy did - dle - o - day.

2. "Hi," said the blackbird, sitting on a chair,
"Once I courted a lady fair;
She proved fickle and turned her back,
And ever since then I've dressed in black."
Refrain

3. "Hi," said the woodpecker, sitting in the grass,
"Once I courted a bonny lass;
She proved fickle and from me fled,
And ever since then my head's been red."
Refrain

4. "Hi," said the greenfinch as he flew,
"I loved one that proved untrue;
And since she will no more be seen,
Every spring I change to green."
Refrain

Watch the dynamics in this song. They help to tell the story.

Farmer Jacob

Folk Song from Hungary

Farm-er Ja-cob had a bil-ly goat, 'Till a wolf de-voured him, sil-ly goat! Then he ate farm-er's old nan-ny goat, Now the farm-er has-n't a-ny goat!

Bil-ly goat, sil-ly goat! Then he ate the farm-er's nan-ny goat, Now the farm-er has-n't a-ny goat!

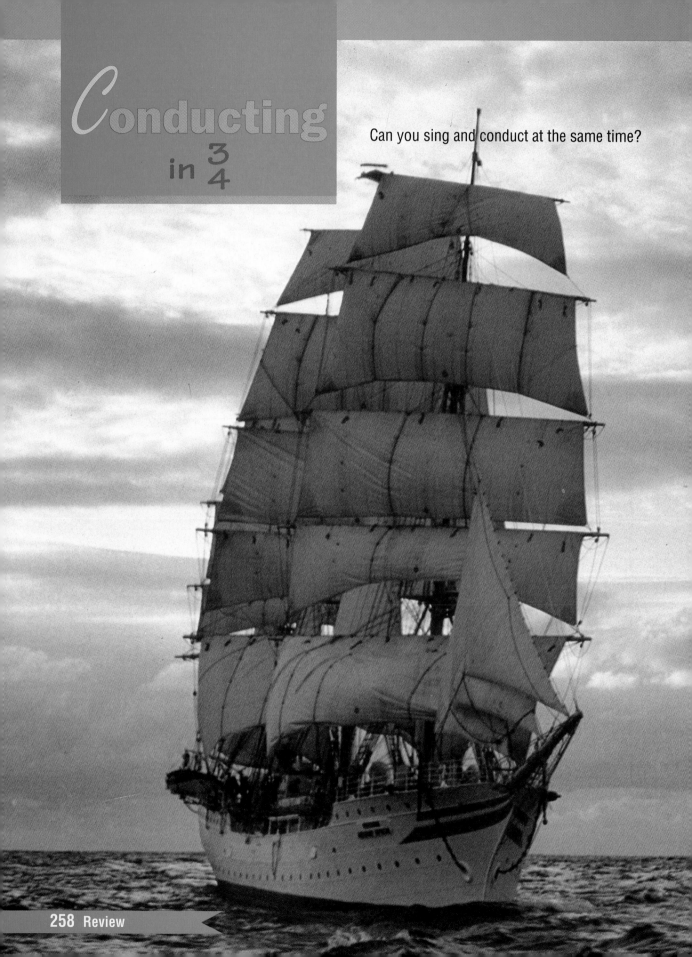

Conducting in $\frac{3}{4}$

Can you sing and conduct at the same time?

Farewell to Tarwathie

Folk Song from Scotland

1. Fare - well to Tar - wa - thie, A - dieu Mor - mond Hill,

And the dear land of Crim - mond, I bid thee fare - well.

I'm bound out for Green - land and read - y to sail,

In ___ hopes to find rich - es in hunt - ing the whale.

2. Farewell to my comrades for a while I must part,
   And likewise the dear lass who first won my heart,
   The cold coast of Greenland my heart will not chill,
   The longer the absence the more loving she'll feel.

3. Our ship is well rigged and she's ready to sail,
   The crew, they are anxious to follow the whale.
   Where the icebergs do float and the stormy winds blow,
   Where the land and the ocean is covered with snow.

4. The cold coast of Greenland is barren and bare,
   No seedling nor harvest is ever known there,
   And the birds here sing sweetly in mountain and vale,
   But there's no bird in Greenland to sing to the whale.

A Ballad from England

How does the scale used in this song reflect the mood of the story told?

The Fox

Folk Song from England

1. The fox went out on a stor-my night, And prayed to the moon to give him light, He'd a long, long way to tra-vel that night be- fore he reached his den, oh! Den, oh! Den, __ oh! He'd a long, long way to tra-vel that night be - fore he reached his den, oh!

2. At last he came to a farmer's yard,
   Where the ducks and geese were all afeared.
   "The best of you all shall grease my beard,
   Before I leave the town, oh!
   Town, oh! Town, oh!" *(repeat lines 3 and 4)*

3. He took the gray goose by the neck,
   He laid a duck across his back,
   And heeded not their quack! quack! quack!
   With the legs all dangling down, oh!
   Down, oh! Down, oh!" *(repeat lines 3 and 4)*

4. Then old mother Slipper Slopper jumped
   out of bed
   And out of the window she popped her head.
   Crying, "John, John! The gray goose is dead,
   And the fox is over the down, oh!
   Down, oh! Down, oh!" *(repeat lines 3 and 4)*

5. Then John got up to the top of the hill,
   And blew his horn both loud and shrill,
   "Blow on," said Reynard, "your music still,
   Whilst I trot home to my den, oh!
   Den, oh! Den, oh!" *(repeat lines 3 and 4)*

What kinds of pictures do the words of this song create in your mind?

Barb'ry Allen

Folk Song from England

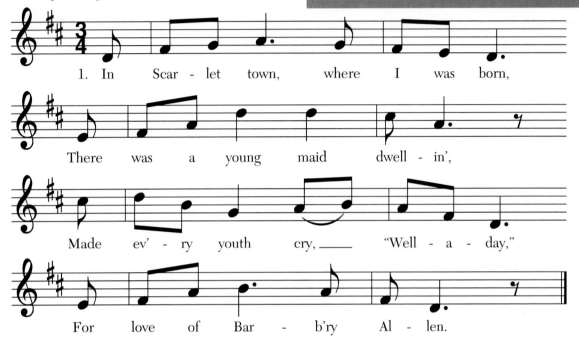

1. In Scar-let town, where I was born,
There was a young maid dwell-in',
Made ev'-ry youth cry, ____ "Well-a-day,"
For love of Bar-b'ry Al-len.

2. 'Twas in the merry month of May,
When green buds they were swellin',
Sweet William on his deathbed lay,
For love of Barb'ry Allen.

3. He sent his servant to the town,
To the place where she was dwellin',
Cried, "Master bids you come to him,
If your name be Barb'ry Allen."

4. Then slowly, slowly she got up,
And slowly went she nigh him,
And when she pulled the curtains back
Said, "Young man, I think you're dyin'."

5. "Oh, yes, I'm sick, I'm very sick,
And I never will be better,
Until I have the love of one,
The love of Barb'ry Allen."

6. Then lightly tripped she down the stairs,
She trembled like an aspen.
"'Tis vain, 'tis vain, my dear young man,
To long for Barb'ry Allen."

7. She walked out in the green, green fields,
She heard his death bells knellin'.
And every stroke they seemed to say;
"Hard-hearted Barb'ry Allen."

8. "Oh, father, father, dig my grave,
Go dig it deep and narrow.
Sweet William died for me today;
I'll die for him tomorrow."

9. They buried her in the old churchyard,
Sweet William's grave was nigh her,
And from his heart grew a red, red rose,
And from her heart a brier.

10. They grew and grew o'er the old church wall,
'Till they could grow no higher,
Until they tied a lover's knot,
The red rose and the brier.

Singing a Round

You and your classmates can perform this song as a round or as a **quodlibet**, in which each group repeats one line over and over.

King of Portugal and John of Gaunt *Anon*

Welcome, Welcome, Every Guest

Traditional Round

I

Wel-come, wel-come, ev - 'ry guest,   Wel-come to our   mu - sic fest,

II

Mu - sic   is   our   on - ly __ cheer,   Fills both soul   and _   ra - vished ear,

III

Sa - cred muse, _ teach   us   the road,   Sweet-est notes to __   be   ex-plored,

IV

Soft - ly swell the   trem - bling _ air,   To __ com-plete our _   con - cert fare.

Courtesy of Sacred Harp Publishing Co., Inc.

The Wraggle-Taggle Gypsies

Old Ballad from England

1. There — were three gyp - sies a - come to my door,
2. Then — she pulled off her — silk fin - ished gown,

And down - stairs ran this — la - dy, O!
And put on hose of — leath - er, O!

The first sang high and the sec - ond sang low,
The rag - ged rags a - bout — our door,

And the third sang "Bon - ny, bon - ny Bis - cay, O!"
And she's gone with the wrag - gle - tag - gle gyp - sies, O!

3. It was late last night when my lord came home,
   Inquiring for his lady, O!
   The servants said on ev'ry hand,
   "She's gone with the wraggle-taggle gypsies, O!"

4. "Come, saddle to me my milk-white steed,
   And go and seek my pony, O!
   That I may ride and seek my bride,
   Who is gone with the wraggle-taggle gypsies, O!"

5. Then he rode high, and he rode low,
   He rode through wood and copses too.
   Until he came to an open field,
   And there he espied his a-lady, O!

Two Versions of a *Song*

Both of these versions are **parodies** of a well-known song.

Little Tom Tinker   Version 1

Traditional Round

Ti - ny Tom-my Tink - er was en - sconced up - on   a clink - er and com-

menced to lac-ri-mate,   "Ma-ter! Ma-ter! See me in my poor, pa-thet-ic state!"

Little Tom Tinker   Version 2

Traditional Round

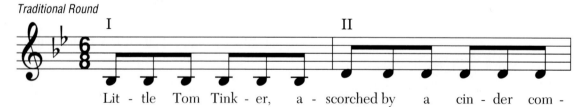

Lit - tle Tom Tink - er,   a - scorched by   a   cin - der com-

bus-tive, did la - ment,   "Fe-male par - ent! I'm such a pit-e-ous gent!"

What is different about the notes in the color boxes?

One Morning in May

Folk Song from the Appalachian Mountains

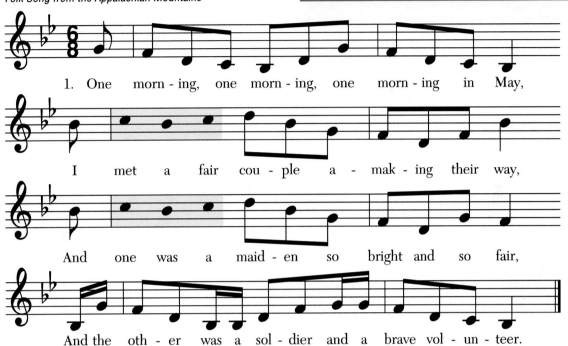

1. One morn - ing, one morn - ing, one morn - ing in May,
I met a fair cou - ple a - mak - ing their way,
And one was a maid - en so bright and so fair,
And the oth - er was a sol - dier and a brave vol - un - teer.

2. "Good morning, good morning, good morning to thee,
O where are you going my pretty lady?"
"O I am a-going to the banks of the sea,
To see the waters gliding, hear the nightingale sing."

3. We hadn't been standing but a minute or two
When out from his knapsack a fiddle he drew,
And the tune that he played made the valleys all ring,
O see the waters gliding, hear the nightingale sing.

4. "Pretty soldier, pretty soldier, will you marry me?"
"O no, pretty lady, that never can be;
I've a wife in old London and children twice three;
Two wives and the army's too many for me."

5. "I'll go back to London and stay there one year
And often I'll think of you, my little dear,
If ever I return, 'twill be in the spring
To see the waters gliding, hear the nightingale sing."

A Song of the Sea

Skye Boat Song

Words by Sir Harold Boulton   Music by Annie MacLeod

A REFRAIN

Speed, bon - nie boat, like a bird on the wing;

"On - ward," the sail - ors cry.

Car - ry the lad that's born to be king,

Fine

O - ver the sea to Skye.

B VERSE

1. Loud the winds howl, loud the waves roar,
2. Tho' the waves leap, soft shall ye sleep,

Thun - der - clouds rend the air;
O - cean's a roy - al bed.

Baf - fled, our foes stand by the shore;
Rock'd in the deep, Flo - ra will keep

D.C. al Fine

Fol - low they will not dare.
Watch by your wea - ry head.

What things in this song are opposites?

Nottamun Town

Folk Song from England

1. As I rode out _____ in Not-ta-mun Town, _____

Not a soul would look up, _____ Not a soul would look down, _____

Not a soul would look up, _____ Not a soul would look down, _____

To show me the way to fair Not-ta-mun Town. _____

2. I rode a gray horse that was called a gray mare,
   With a gray mane and tail, green stripe down her back,
   Gray mane and gray tail, green stripe down her back,
   There was no hair on her that wasn't coal black.

3. She stood so still, she threw me to the dirt,
   She tore my hide and bruised my shirt,
   From saddle to stirrup I mounted again
   And on my ten toes I rode over the plain.

4. Met the King and the Queen and a company more,
   A-riding behind and a-marching before;
   Come a strange looking drummer a-beating a drum,
   With his hands in his pockets come marching along.

New Rhythm

Sing this melody at sight. Perform the notes in the color boxes *unevenly*.

Cardigan Bay   *John Brett*

What type of wind does the rhythm of this song suggest—fierce or gentle? Can you find the new rhythm?

A Sailor's Song

Blow the Wind Southerly

Folk Song from Northumbria

A

Blow the wind south - er - ly, south - er - ly, south - er - ly,

Blow the wind south o'er the bon - ny blue sea;

Blow the wind south - er - ly, south - er - ly, south - er - ly,

Fine

Blow, bon - ny breeze, __ my true love to me.

B

1. He told me last night there were ships in the off - ing,
2. I stood by the light - house that last time we part - ed,

And I hur - ried down to the deep roll - ing sea;
'Till dark - ness came down o'er the deep roll - ing sea;

But my eye could not see it, wher - ev - er might be it,
And no long - er I saw the bright bark of my true ___

D.C. al Fine

The bark that is bear - ing my true love to me.
love, Blow bon - ny breeze ___ and bring him to me.

Play this song on recorder. Will you have to learn any new notes?

Keeping Watch

Little Boy of the Sheep

English Words by Alice Firgau   *Folk Song from the Hebrides Islands*

Sing me a song, pipe me a tune,

Guard the sheep well, O shep - herd boy.

Keep - ing the sheep all day, watch - ing they do not stray

O - ver the hill - side, O shep - herd boy.

From FOLKSONGS AND FOLKLORE OF THE SOUTH UIST. Used by permission of Margaret Fay Shaw.

Sonata in A Major

Wolfgang A. Mozart

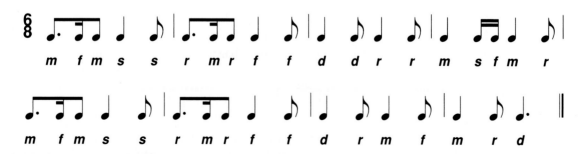

m f m s   s r m r f   f d   d r   r m   s f m   r

m f m s   s r m r f   f d   r m   f m   r d

A Famous Folk Song

This well-known song has been passed on from one generation to another.

Hermitage, St. Petersburg.
Photo: The Bridgeman Art Library, London.

Greensleeves

16th-Century Folk Song from England

The Musicians   *Anon*

1. A - las, my love, — you do me wrong _to cast   me off __ dis-cour-teous-ly;
2. My men were cloth - ed all in green And they   did ev - er wait on thee;

And I have lov - ed you so long, De - light - ing in ___ your com-pa - ny.
All this was gal - lant to be seen, And yet __ thou wouldst _not love _ me.

REFRAIN

Green - sleeves _ was all my joy, ___ Green - sleeves _ was my de-light,

Green - sleeves was my heart of gold, _ And who but my La - dy Green - sleeves?

Old Texas

Cowboy Song from Oklahoma

1. I'm goin' to leave ___(echo)___ old __ Tex - as now, (echo)

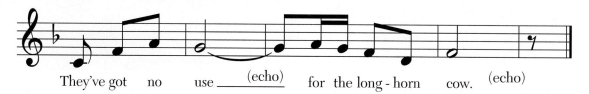

They've got no use ___(echo)___ for the long - horn cow. (echo)

Springfield Mountain

Folk Song from the United States

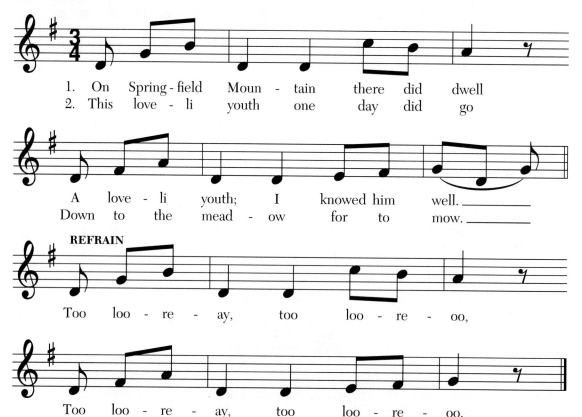

1. On Spring - field Moun - tain there did dwell
2. This love - li youth one day did go

A love - li youth; I knowed him well. ___
Down to the mead - ow for to mow. ___

REFRAIN

Too loo - re - ay, too loo - re - oo,

Too loo - re - ay, too loo - re - oo.

Prepare a performance of this song by adding as many parts as you can.

Rock-a My Soul

African American Spiritual

1. Rock - a my soul — in the bo - som of A - bra - ham,

Rock - a my soul — in the bo - som of A - bra - ham,

Rock - a my soul — in the bo - som of A - bra - ham,

Oh, rock - a my soul.

2. So high, you can't get over it,
So low, you can't get under it,
So wide, you can't get around it,
You gotta go in at the door.

Choose a key that is comfortable for your voice.

Love Somebody

Folk Song from the United States

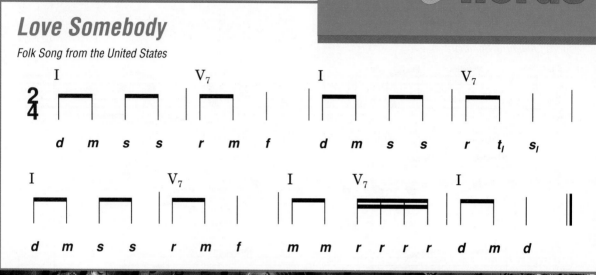

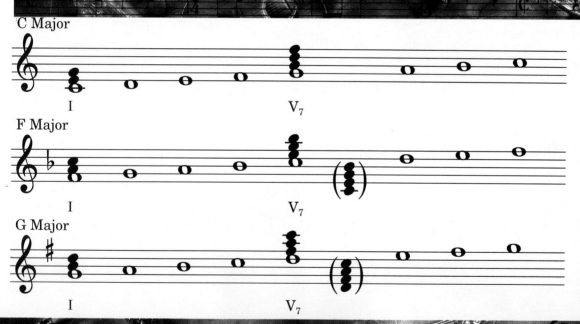

C Major

I   V₇

F Major

I   V₇

G Major

I   V₇

Can you remember the words to these songs?

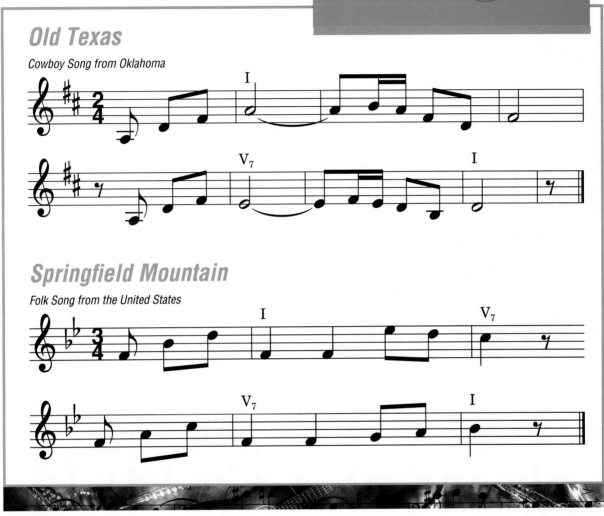

Old Texas

Cowboy Song from Oklahoma

Springfield Mountain

Folk Song from the United States

/ntervals

Whether you count up or down, the interval is still the same.

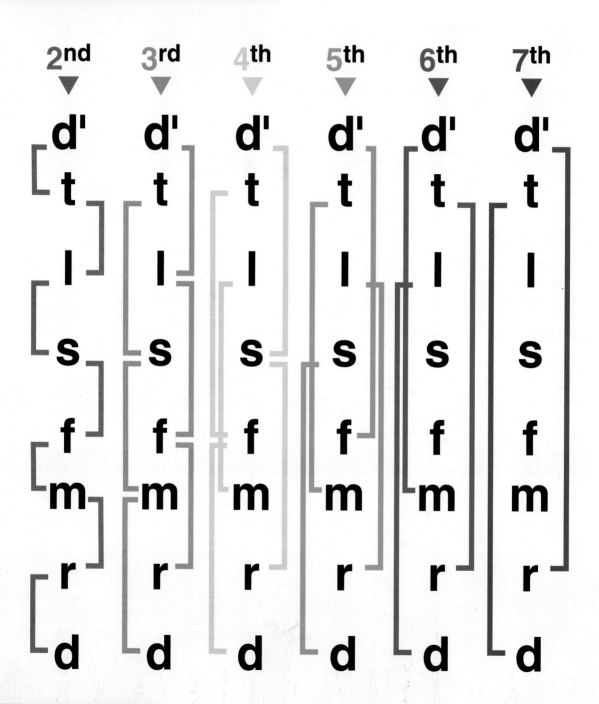

2nd	3rd	4th	5th	6th	7th
d'	d'	d'	d'	d'	d'
t	t	t	t	t	t
l	l	l	l	l	l
s	s	s	s	s	s
f	f	f	f	f	f
m	m	m	m	m	m
r	r	r	r	r	r
d	d	d	d	d	d

How many chords do you need to play this song?

Practicing Chords

When the Saints Go Marching In

African American Spiritual

1. Oh, when the   saints ___ go march-ing   in, ___   Oh, when the

saints   go   march-ing   in, ___   Oh, Lord I   want   to   be   in that

num - ber ___ When the   saints   go   march - ing   in.

2. Oh, when the stars refuse to shine, . . .   3. Oh, when I hear that trumpet sound, . . .

Under the Stars

I Wonder As I Wander

Collected by John Jacob Niles

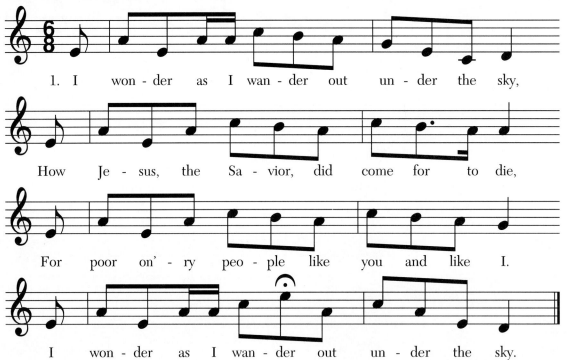

1. I won-der as I wan-der out un-der the sky,
How Je-sus, the Sa-vior, did come for to die,
For poor on'-ry peo-ple like you and like I.
I won-der as I wan-der out un-der the sky.

2. When Mary birthed Jesus, 'twas in a cow's stall,
With wise men and farmers and shepherds and all.
But high from the heavens a star's light did fall,
And the promise of ages it then did recall.

Two Songs About Friendship

Hineh Mah Tov *(How Good the Time)*

Round from Israel

Hi - neh mah tov u - mah na - yim She - vet a -
How good and pleas - ant it is for broth - ers to

chim gam ya - chad. Hi - neh mah _____
dwell to - geth - er. Good and pleas -

tov _____ She - vet a - chim gam ya - chad.
ant for broth - ers to dwell to - geth - er.

Auld Lang Syne

Poem by Robert Burns   Traditional Tune from Scotland

1. Should auld ac-quaint-ance be for-got, And ne - ver brought to mind?
2. And here's a hand, my trust-y friend, And give us a hand of thine,

Should auld ac-quaint-ance be for-got, And days of auld lang syne?
We'll take a cup of kind-ness yet, For auld _ lang _ syne.

REFRAIN

For auld _ lang _ syne, my dear, For auld _ lang _ syne,

We'll take a cup of kind-ness yet, For auld _ lang _ syne.

What do the Roman numerals above
the music mean?

A Melody *from* Africa

Kum Ba Yah

Traditional Song from Africa

REFRAIN

I   IV   I

Kum   ba   yah,   my   Lord,   Kum   ba   yah!

I   V₇

Kum   ba   yah,   my   Lord,   Kum   ba   yah!

I   IV   I

Kum   ba   yah,   my   Lord,   Kum   ba   yah!

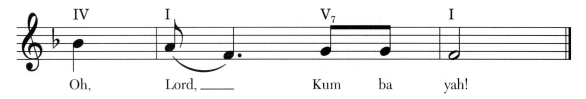

IV   I   V₇   I

Oh,   Lord, _____   Kum   ba   yah!

1. Someone's singin', ...   2. Someone's prayin', ...   3. Someone's shoutin', ...

What instrument would sound best accompanying this song?

A Cowboy Song

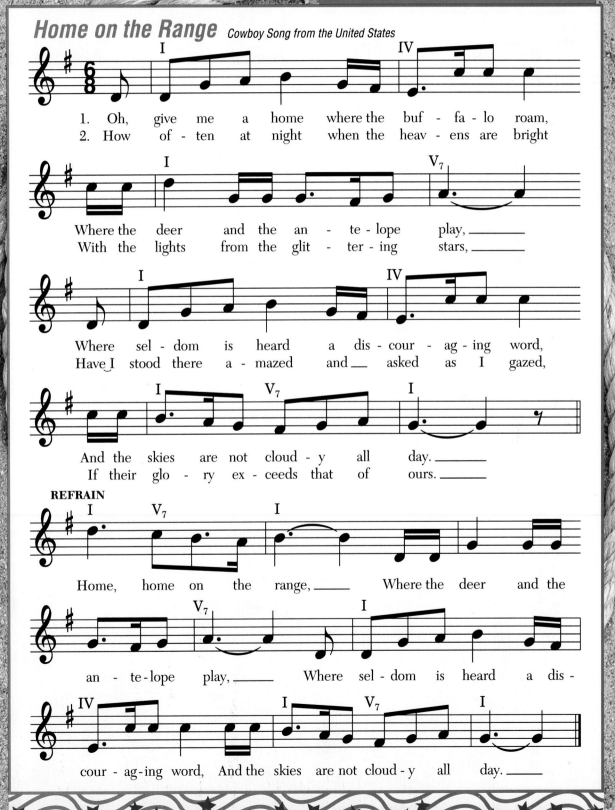

Home on the Range
Cowboy Song from the United States

1. Oh, give me a home where the buf - fa - lo roam,
2. How of - ten at night when the heav - ens are bright

Where the deer and the an - te - lope play, _____
With the lights from the glit - ter - ing stars, _____

Where sel - dom is heard a dis - cour - ag - ing word,
Have I stood there a - mazed and __ asked as I gazed,

And the skies are not cloud - y all day. _____
If their glo - ry ex - ceeds that of ours. _____

REFRAIN

Home, home on the range, _____ Where the deer and the

an - te - lope play, _____ Where sel - dom is heard a dis -

cour - ag - ing word, And the skies are not cloud - y all day. _____

Which lines of music in this song look similar?

Deep in the Heart of Texas

Words by June Hershey   Music by Don Swander

The stars at night are big and bright, Deep in the heart of Tex-as; ____

The prai-rie sky is wide and high, Deep in the heart of Tex-as. ____

The sage in bloom is like per-fume, Deep in the heart of Tex-as; ____

Re-minds me of the one I love, Deep in the heart of Tex-as. ____

Get On Board

New River Train

Folk Song from the United States

1. I'm rid-in' on that New Riv-er train,_____
2. 𝄽 Dar - lin', you can't love ____ one,_____
3. 𝄽 Dar - lin', you can't love ____ two,_____

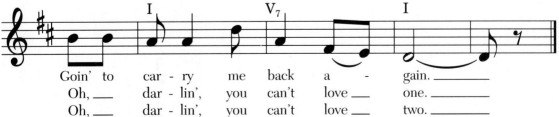

I'm rid-in' on that New Riv-er train.
𝄽 Dar - lin', you can't love ____ one;_____
𝄽 Dar - lin', you can't love ____ two;_____

Same old train that brought me ____ here
You can't love one and have an - y fun,
You can't love two and still be ____ true,

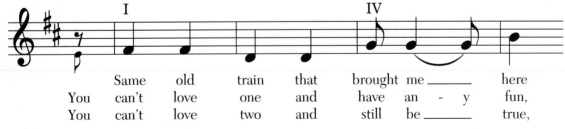

Goin' to car - ry me back a - gain. ____
Oh, ____ dar - lin', you can't love ____ one. ____
Oh, ____ dar - lin', you can't love ____ two. ____

4. Darlin', you can't love three, . . .
   You can't love three
   and still love me . . .

5. Darlin', you can't love four, . . .
   You can't love four,
   make it up if you want more . . .

Do songs necessarily sound different
if they look different?

Old Dan Tucker

Folk Song from the United States

VERSE

1. Old Dan Tuck-er was a might-y man, He washed his face in the fry-ing pan,

Combed his hair with a wag-on wheel, Had a tooth-ache in his heel;

REFRAIN

So get out the way, Old Dan Tuck-er; Get out the way, Old Dan Tuck-er;

Get out the way, Old Dan Tuck-er, You're too late to get your sup-per.

2. Old Dan Tucker came to town,
Riding a billy goat, leading a hound;
Hound dog barked, then billy goat jumped;
Dan fell off and landed on a stump; *Refrain*

Why were early sailors so concerned about the wind?

An American Shanty

Blow, Ye Winds

Folk Song from the United States

1. 'Tis ad-ver-tised in Bos-ton, New York, and Buf-fa-lo,
2. They send you to New Bed-ford, that fa-mous whal-ing port,

Five hun-dred brave A-mer-i-cans, a-whal-ing for to go. __
And give you to some land sharks __ to board and fit you out. __

REFRAIN

Sing-ing, "Blow, ye winds in the morn-ing, And blow, ye winds, high - O!

Clear a-way your run-ning gear, And blow, ye winds, high - O!"

3. It's now we're out to sea, my boys,
   the wind begins to blow,
   One half the watch is sick on deck
   and the other half below. *Refrain*

4. The skipper's on the quarter-deck
   a-squinting at the sails,
   When up aloft the look-out sights
   a school of whales. *Refrain*

5. "Now clear away the boats, my boys,
   and after him we'll trail,
   But if you get too near to him,
   he'll kick you with his tail!" *Refrain*

6. Now we've got him turned up,
   we tow him alongside;
   We over with our blubber hooks
   and rob him of his hide. *Refrain*

7. Next comes the stowing down, my boys;
   'twill take both night and day,
   And you'll all have fifty cents apiece
   when you collect your pay. *Refrain*

From SONGS OF SAILORMEN by Joanna C. Colcord. Used courtesy W. W. Norton & Co.

A Two-Part Song

This song can be played as a duet. For your part, use a recorder or any instrument you like.

The Water Is Wide
Folk Song from England

Countermelody

Melody

The wa-ter is wide, _____ I can't get
There is a __ ship _____ sailing on the
Oh, love is __ hand - some and love is

1. The wa-ter is wide, _____ I can-not get o'er,
2. There is a __ ship _____ sail-ing on the sea,
3. Oh, love is __ handsome _____ and __ love is fine,

o'er, And I've no __ wings, _____ No wings to
sea, She's load-ed __ deep _____ as deep can
fine, And love is __ charm - ing when it is

And nei-ther have _____ I wings to __ fly,
She's load-ed deep _____ as deep can _ be,
And love is charm - ing when it is true,

Harmony in Thirds

When harmony is in thirds, both notes are on a line or both are in a space.

Can you find any places in this music where the harmony is *not* in thirds?

A Lullaby from Indonesia

Suliram

English Words by Marc Merson   *Folk Song from Indonesia*

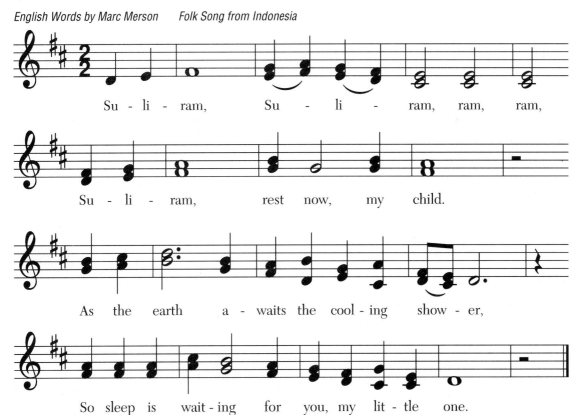

Su - li - ram, Su - li - ram, ram, ram,

Su - li - ram, rest now, my child.

As the earth a - waits the cool - ing show - er,

So sleep is wait - ing for you, my lit - tle one.

Can you find the notes of this song on the keyboard?

Ezekiel Saw the Wheel

African American Spiritual

E - ze-kiel saw the wheel, 'Way up in the mid-dle of the air,

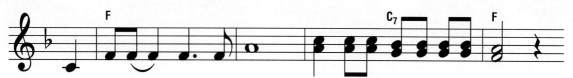

E - ze-kiel saw the wheel, 'Way in the mid-dle of the air.

Now the big wheel turn by faith, And the lit - tle wheel turn by the

grace of God, It's a wheel in a wheel, 'Way in the mid-dle of the air.

1. Some go to church for to sing and shout, 'Way in the mid-dle of the air,
2. One of these days 'bout twelve o'-clock, 'Way in the mid-dle of the air,

Be - fore six months they're shout-ed out! 'Way in the mid-dle of the air.
⁊ This old world gonna reel and rock! 'Way in the mid-dle of the air.

Use your ear to tell you what the missing notes sound like.

Minka

Words by Louise Ayres Garnett　　*Folk Melody from Russia*

From the Vol - ga　I　was rid - ing,　On　my great horse no - bly strid - ing,

When　I　saw　in　sha - dow hid - ing,　Min - ka, charm-ing　Min - ka.

Min - ka,　Min - ka,　I　have spied thee,　Do　not　in　the　for - est hide thee,

On　your white horse ride　be - side　me,　Min - ka, charm-ing　Min - ka.

A Snow-White Bird

English Words by Jean Sinor   Folk Song from Flanders

1. A snow - white bird sang in a tree,

A snow - white bird sang in a tree,

He sang his sweet-est song for me, non - ny, non - ny no.

He sang his sweet-est song for me, non - ny no.

2. Oh, tell me, tell me, little bird,
   Oh, tell me, tell me, little bird,
   Is it my true love's song you've heard? Nonny, nonny no.
   Is it my true love's song you've heard? Nonny no.

3. More sadly sang the snow-white dove,
   More sadly sang the snow-white dove,
   For he was mourning for his love, nonny, nonny no.
   For he was mourning for his love, nonny no.

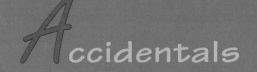

How do sharps, flats, and natural signs change notes?

With your classmates, sing this song as a round.
The second part starts after two beats.

Joshua Fought the Battle of Jericho

African American Spiritual

A Song to Perform

Try playing this song on recorder and then on keyboard.

Shake Hands, Mary

African American Children's Song

From PLAY SONGS OF THE DEEP SOUTH by Altona Trent-Johns. Copyright by Association for the Study of Afro-American Life and History, Inc. Used by permission.

You can accompany this
song using only two chords.

Chords

The Miller of Dee

Folk Song from England

1. There was a jol-ly mil-ler once lived on the riv-er Dee,

He sang and danced from morn to night, no lark as blithe as he,

And _ this the bur-den of his song for-ev-er used to be, ____

I care for no-bod-y, no, not I, and no-bod-y cares for me.

2. So let us his example take,
   And be from malice free,
   Let everyone his neighbor serve
   As served he'd like to be.
   And merrily pass the tray around
   And dance and sing with glee,
   If nobody cares a fig for us,
   Why not a fig care we.

A Prince of a Song

"Skye Boat Song" on page 266 tells about the famous Bonnie Prince Charlie. Here is another song that explains why he is a hero in Scotland.

Charlie Is My Darling

Folk Song from Scotland

Oh, Char - lie is my dar - ling, my dar - ling, my dar - ling,

Oh, Char - lie is my dar - ling, the young chev - a - lier.

1. 'Twas on a Mon - day morn - ing, right ear - ly in the year,

When Char - lie came to our ___ house, the ___ young ___ chev - a - lier.

2. As he came marching up the street, the pipes played loud and clear,
   And the folk came running out to meet the young chevalier. *Refrain*

3. With Highland bonnets on their heads, and claymores bright and clear,
   They came to fight for Scotland's right and the young chevalier. *Refrain*

A New Scale

Does this song sound mostly major or mostly minor?

Carrion Crow

Folk Song from Nova Scotia

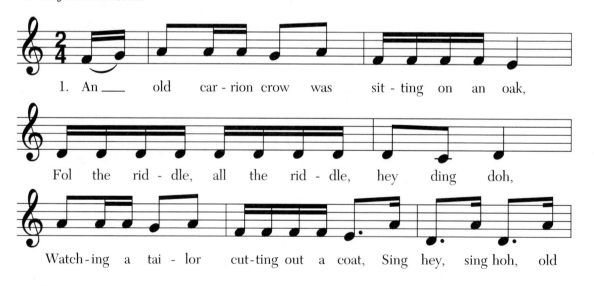

1. An ___ old car - rion crow was sit - ting on an oak,

Fol the rid - dle, all the rid - dle, hey ding doh,

Watch - ing a tai - lor cut - ting out a coat, Sing hey, sing hoh, old

From TRADITIONAL SONGS FROM NOVA SCOTIA by Helen Creighton. Reprinted by permission of McGraw-Hill-Reyerson Limited.

car - rion crow, Fol the rid - dle, all the rid - dle, hey ding doh.

REFRAIN

Ki - mi -lea - ro Ki - mi - lea - ro, Ki - mi -lea - ro Ki - mo, To me

hump, bump, bump, jump Pol-ly wol-ly lee, Lin - ko kil -ly cum Ki - mo.

2. Wife, oh wife, bring me my
cross and bow, . . .
That I may shoot yon carrion
crow. . . .
Refrain

3. Oh, the tailor shot and missed
his mark, . . .
And he shot the miller's sow
right through the heart. . . .
Refrain

Ancient Melody

This melody has been used by many composers over the years.

Greensleeves

16th-Century Folk Song from England

1. A - las, my love, _ you do me wrong _ to cast me off ____ dis-cour-teous-ly;
2. My men were cloth - ed all in green _ And they did ev - er wait on thee;

And I have lov - ed you so long, _ De - light-ing in _____ your com - pa - ny.
All this was gal - lant to be seen, _ And yet _ thou wouldst _ not love _ me.

REFRAIN

Green - sleeves _ was all my joy, _____ Green - sleeves _ was my de-light,

Green-sleeves was my heart of gold, _ And who but my La - dy Green-sleeves?

The Natural Sign

Can you tell what a natural sign shows?

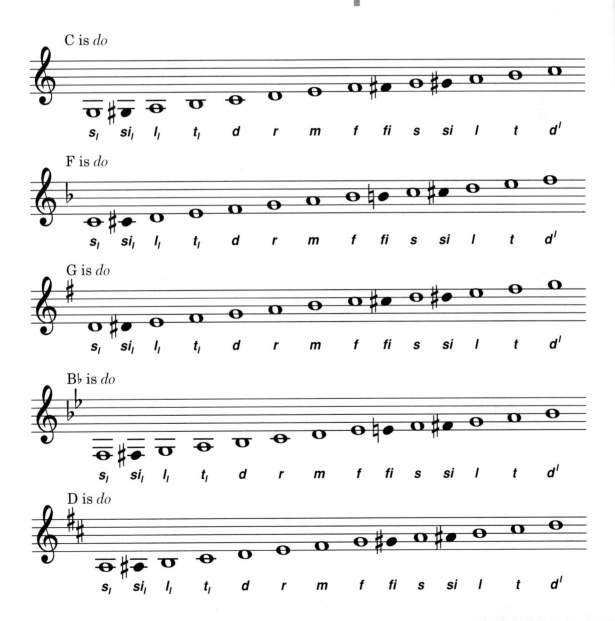

How do *fa* and *fi* show what the next note probably is?

Grasshoppers Three

Traditional

Melody

d d d d | r m d d d | f m

Grass-hop-pers three a - fid - dl - ing went; Hey! Ho!

r s, s, s, | s, d | d d d r m | f s s

nev - er be still; They paid no mon-ey to - ward their rent, But

l l s s | fi fi s | s d d d d r

all day long with el - bows bent They fid-dled a tune called

m m m m f s | d d d d | r m d d d

ril - la - by, ril - la - by, Fid-dled a tune called ril - la - by - ril.

Countermelody

d | s, l, t, d | s, d t, l, | s,

Hey! ril - la - by ril, ril - la - by, Hey! Ho!

f, | s, l, t, d | s, l, t, d t, l, s, | m,

Hey! ril - la - by, Ho! ril - la - by ril - la - by ril, but

f, m, | r, s, l, t, d | s, l, t,

all day long fid - dled a tune, ril - la - by,

d t, l, | s, l, | s, l, t, d | s, d

ril - la - by, Oh Hey! ril - la - by ril - la - by.

What song do you think this is?

3

| s | m | d | m | s | d' | | m' | r' | d' | m | fi | s |

| s | s | m' | r' | d' | t | | l | t | d' | d' | s | m | d |

| s | m | d | m | s | d' | | m' | r' | d' | m | fi | s |

| s | s | m' | r' | d' | t | | l | t | d' | d' | s | m | d |

| m' | m' | m' | f' | s' | s' | | f' | m' | r' | m' | f' | f' |

| f' | m' | r' | d' | t | | l | t | d' | m | fi | s |

| s | d' | d' | d' | t | l | l | l | r' | f' | m' | r' | d' | d' | t |

| s | s | d' | r' | m' | f' | s' | | d' | r' | m' | f' | r' | d' |

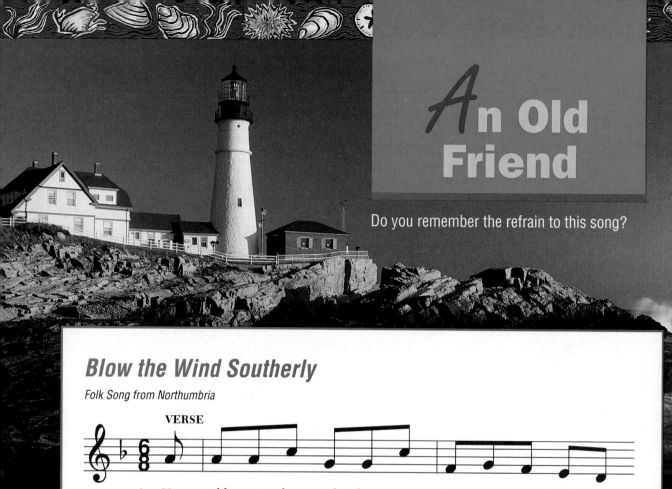

An Old Friend

Do you remember the refrain to this song?

Blow the Wind Southerly

Folk Song from Northumbria

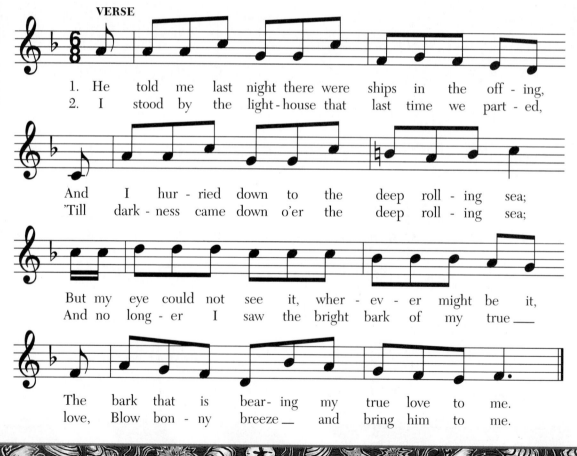

VERSE

1. He told me last night there were ships in the off-ing,
2. I stood by the light-house that last time we part-ed,

And I hur-ried down to the deep roll-ing sea;
'Till dark-ness came down o'er the deep roll-ing sea;

But my eye could not see it, wher-ev-er might be it,
And no long-er I saw the bright bark of my true___

The bark that is bear-ing my true love to me.
love, Blow bon-ny breeze___ and bring him to me.

In *Praise of* Beauty

What key is this song in?

Yonder Stands a Handsome Lady

Folk Song from the United States

1. Yon-der _ stands a _ hand-some la - dy, Who she _ is I _ do not _ know,

Shall I _ court her for her beau-ty, What says you, _ ma-dam, yes or no?

2. Madam, I have gold and silver
   Madam, I have house and land,
   Madam, I have a world of treasure,
   And all shall be at your command.

3. Madam, do not count on beauty,
   Beauty is a flower that will soon decay,
   The brightest flower in the midst of summer
   In the fall it will fade away.

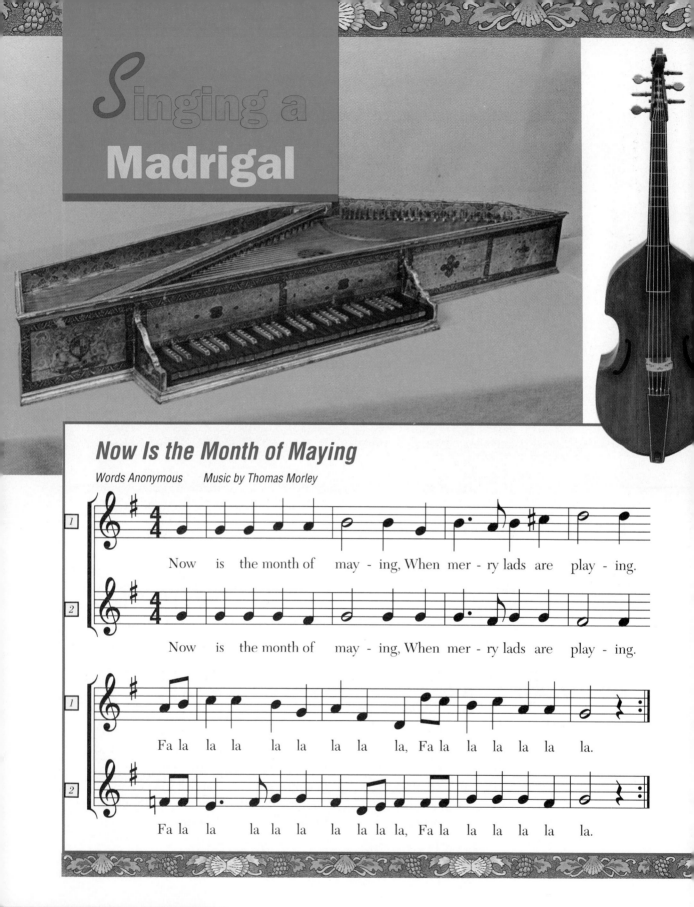

Singing a Madrigal

Now Is the Month of Maying

Words Anonymous *Music by Thomas Morley*

Now is the month of may - ing, When mer - ry lads are play - ing.

Now is the month of may - ing, When mer - ry lads are play - ing.

Fa la la la la la la la, Fa la la la la la la.

Fa la la la la la la la la, Fa la la la la la la.

Madrigals were very popular during the sixteenth century. What instrument would you play to accompany this song?

[1] Each with his bon - ny lass, Up - on the green - y grass,

[2] Each with his bon - ny lass, Up - on the green - y grass,

[1] Fa la la la la, Fa la la la la la la la, Fa la la la.

[2] Fa la la la la, Fa la la la la, Fa la la la la la la.

A Great Composer

 Symphony No. 94,
Movement 2 (excerpt)
..........Franz Joseph Haydn

l, l, d d m m d r r t, t, si, si, m, etc.

Meet the Composer

Franz Joseph Haydn was born in a small village in Austria. When just a little boy, he would pretend to play the violin with two pieces of wood as he listened to his mother sing folk songs.

When Haydn was twenty-nine years old, a wealthy Hungarian nobleman named Esterházy hired him to write music for his private orchestra. In those days, every castle had its own group of professional musicians. For thirty years, Haydn lived and worked at the Esterházy castle. Although a musician living in a nobleman's house was just a servant, Haydn did not mind. He was a simple man who was grateful for the opportunity to compose and perform music.

Franz Joseph Haydn (1732-1809)

Modes are actually scales. Do you recognize the mode of this song?

Hold the Wind

African American Spiritual

REFRAIN

Hold the wind, — hold the wind, — hold the wind, don't let it blow.

Hold the wind, — hold the wind, — hold the wind, don't let it blow.

VERSE

1. You may talk a - bout me just as much as you please.

Hold the wind, don't let it blow, I'm gon - na

talk a - bout you on the bend - in' of my knees,

Hold the wind, don't let it blow.

2. If you don't believe I been redeemed, . . .
   Just follow me down to the Jordan
   stream, . . . *Refrain*

3. My soul got wet in the midnight dew, . . .
   And the morning star was a witness
   too, . . . *Refrain*

A Well-known Song

Is this song in major or in minor?

Every Night When the Sun Goes In

Folk Song from the Southern Appalachians

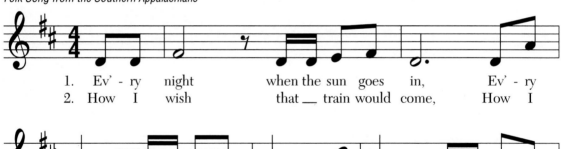

1. Ev' - ry night when the sun goes in, Ev' - ry
2. How I wish that __ train would come, How I

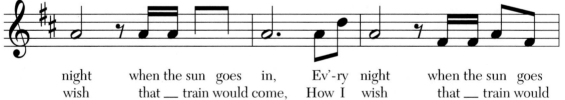

night when the sun goes in, Ev'-ry night when the sun goes
wish that __ train would come, How I wish that __ train would

in, I lay down my head and mourn-ful cry.
come, And take __ me back where I come from.

From SONGS OF THE SOUTHERN APPALACHIANS by Cecil Sharp. Courtesy Oxford University Press.

A Song About...

Using the clues in the song, can you guess what a silkie is? What notes should you sing at the question marks?

The Great Silkie

Folk Song from Scotland

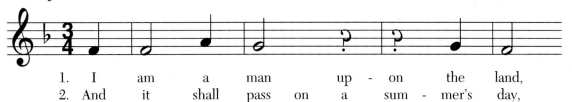

1. I am a man up - on the land,
2. And it shall pass on a sum - mer's day,

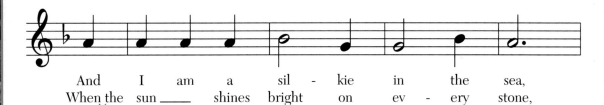

And I am a sil - kie in the sea,
When the sun shines bright on ev - ery stone,

And when I'm far and far from land,
I'll come and fetch my lit - tle son,

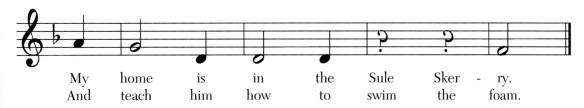

My home is in the Sule Sker - ry.
And teach him how to swim the foam.

A Folk Song Favorite

How is this song similar to "Nottamun Town" on page 267?

Old Joe Clark

Folk Song from the United States   *Words by Raymond Matthews*

VERSE

1. Old Joe Clark, he built a house, Took him 'bout a week;

He built the floors a-bove his head, The ceil-ings un-der his feet.

REFRAIN

Rock - a - rock, Old Joe Clark, Rock - a - rock, I'm gone;

Rock - a - rock, Old Joe Clark, Good-bye, Lu - cy Long.

2. Old Joe Clark, he had a dog
   Like none you've ever seen;
   With floppy ears and curly tail,
   And six feet in between. *Refrain*

3. Old Joe Clark, he had a wife,
   Her name was Betty Sue;
   She had two great big brown eyes,
   The other two were blue. *Refrain*

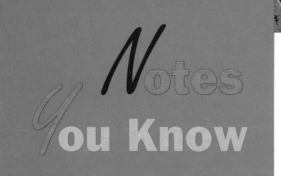

Notes You Know

Here are all of the notes you have studied.

Use this song to practice what you have learned.
You shouldn't have a hard time with the words!

The Alphabet

Attributed to Wolfgang A. Mozart

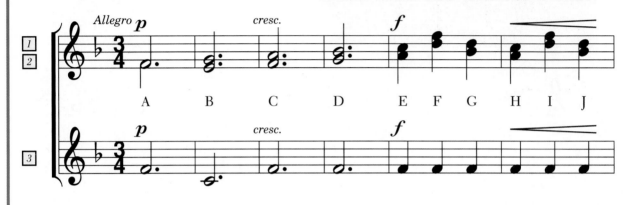

Playing the *Guitar*

There are three basic types of guitars—nylon-string classical, acoustic steel-string, and electric. Learn the names of the parts.

Acoustic steel-string guitar

Electric guitar

Sound hole

Bridge

Nylon-string classical guitar

Tuning a Guitar

In the first stages of playing, your teacher may tune your guitar for you.

You can tune your guitar to the keys of a keyboard. The diagram below shows the pitches for tuning each guitar string.

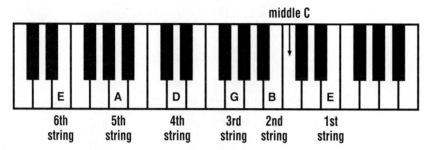

Another possibility is to tune to an inexpensive electronic guitar tuner. Still another way to tune is called relative tuning, described below. When you are ready to tune your own guitar, follow these steps.

1. Tune the sixth, or lowest, string to E on the piano or pitch pipe.

2. Press the sixth string at fret 5. This is the pitch A to which you tune your open fifth string. Pluck the depressed sixth string and the fifth string with your right thumb. When the two sounds match, you are in tune.

3. Press the fifth string at fret 5, and tune the open fourth string to it. Follow the procedure described in step 2.

4. Press the fourth string at fret 5, and tune the open third string to it.

5. Press the third string at fret 4, and tune the open second string to it.

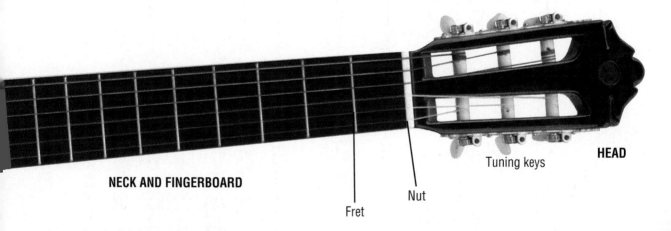

6. Press the second string at fret 5, and tune the open first string to it. Check the low E and the high E. They should be in tune with each other.

7. Have your teacher or an experienced guitar player check your accuracy.

Playing Position

There are several ways to hold your guitar comfortably. The following guidelines will help you be a better player.

- Relax your muscles and avoid tension.

- The guitar neck should be either horizontal or tilted upward (never down).

- Keep the body of the guitar as vertical as possible. Try not to slant the top of the guitar so you can see better. This puts your left hand in a bad position.

Left-hand fingers are numbered 1 through 4. (Pianists: The thumb is not number 1.) Place the thumb in back of the neck, and arch your fingers. Never hold the neck like a baseball bat with the palm against the back.

Your right-hand thumb will strum the strings by brushing across them in a downward motion.

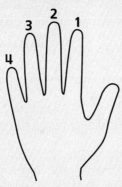

How to Read Guitar Chord Diagrams

A guitar chord diagram shows you

- the **chord name**
- **strings 6** (bass) through **1** (treble)
- the **nut**
- the **frets**
- **left-hand fingers**
- **open** (o) **strings**
- **strings not strummed** (x)

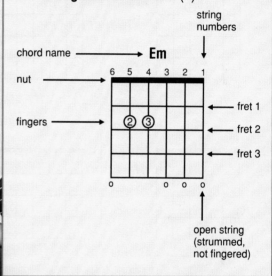

Chords Used in This Book

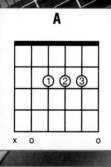

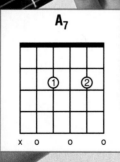

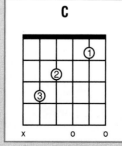

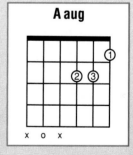

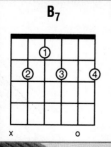

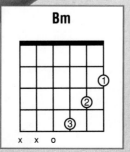

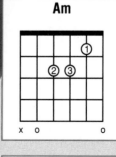

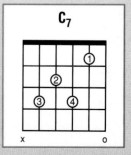

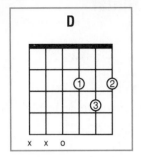

D

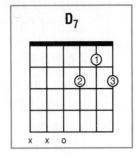

D₇

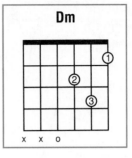

Dm

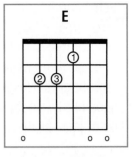

E

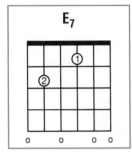

E₇

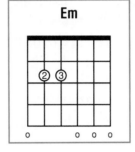

Em

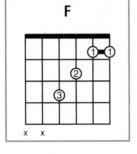

F

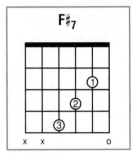

F#₇

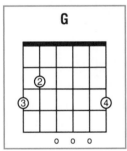

G

or

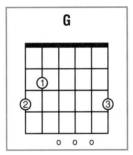

G

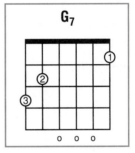

G₇

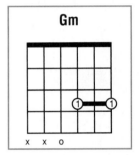

Gm

The Capo

A **capo** (kay-poh) is used to change keys on the guitar. It will make it easy for you to use the guitar to play songs that would otherwise be very difficult. For example, when you see **Guitar: capo 3** on a song with guitar chords, place the capo at the third fret and follow the top set of chord symbols. You will be playing familiar chords in an easy key, but the resulting sounds will match the key in which the song is notated.

Songs to Play on the Guitar

The following songs have guitar accompaniments in this book. Songs are listed by key in alphabetical order. When a capo (see page 320) is needed to play in an easy guitar key, it is indicated after the song title.

Songs in the Key of C
- Annie Lee, page 25
- Free at Last, page 190 (capo 3)
- Hold 'em, Joe, page 86
- Holly and the Ivy, The, page 208 (capo 3)
- Leavin' for Chile *(Cuando pa' Chile me voy)*, page 100
- Little Wheel A-Turnin', page 42 (capo 3)
- Michael, Row the Boat Ashore, page 88 (capo 2)
- Springtime *(La primavera)*, page 112 (capo 3)

Songs in the Key of G
- Bye-Bye, Blues, page 171
- Catch a Falling Star, page 38 (capo 3)
- Charleston, page 165
- Ding-Dong Merrily on High, page 204
- Do, Lord, page 98
- Down the Ohio/Vive L'Amour, pages 36, 37
- Gaudeamus igitur, page 74
- I Got Rhythm, page 143
- Jamaica Farewell, page 12 (capo 5)
- Long John, page 84
- Now Let Me Fly, page 80
- Peace like a River, page 82
- Silent Night, page 203 (capo 3)

Songs in the Key of D
- Abraham, Martin, and John, page 188
- Charlottetown, page 173 (capo 3)
- Cowpoke, The *(El payo)*, page 117 (capo 3)
- Eres tú *(Touch the Wind)*, page 181
- Give a Little Love, page 18
- It's a Good Day, page 64 (capo 1)
- Las mañanitas, page 110 (capo 3)
- Love in Any Language, page 216 (capo 1)
- On the Road Again, page 32
- Swanee, page 138
- Top of the World, page 34

Songs in Minor Keys
- Butterfly, The *(La mariposa)*, page 27 (A minor: capo 2)
- Didn't My Lord Deliver Daniel?, page 92 (E minor)
- Dona Dona, page 174 (A minor: capo 5)
- Hava Nagila, page 158 (G minor)
- My White Horse *(Mi caballo blanco)*, page 15 (A minor: capo 2)
- O Chanukah, page 200 (A minor: capo 5)
- Scarborough Fair, page 70 (A minor: capo 5)
- Song of the Water *(Canto del agua)*, page 124 (E minor)

Using your left hand, cover the holes shown in the first diagram.

Cover the top of the mouthpiece with your lips. Blow gently as you whisper *dahh*. You will be playing G.

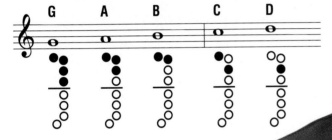

When you can play G, A, and B, you will be able to play a countermelody to accompany "Springfield Mountain."

Practice playing two new notes—high C and high D. When you can play them, you are ready to try another countermelody for "Springfield Mountain."

Learn new notes in pairs: E, D and F, C. Cover the holes securely with your fingers and whisper *dahh* as you play in the low register of the recorder.

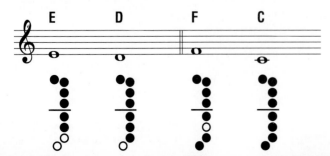

When you can easily play E and D, try playing "Skye Boat Song."

Practice playing F and C. Then try the melody from "Old Dan Tucker."

Follow the Half Step Rule below to play F♯, G♯, and B♭.

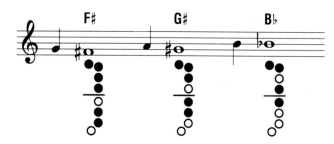

Half Step Rule: To go down a half step from a given pitch, skip a hole and add two holes.

Play F♯ in the melody "Every Night When the Sun Goes In."

You will need G♯ for the melody "A Snow-White Bird."

Review B♭ for a countermelody to "When the Saints Go Marching In."

Fingering Chart

All the recorder notes you will need for melodies, countermelodies, and ostinatos in this book are on the following fingering chart.

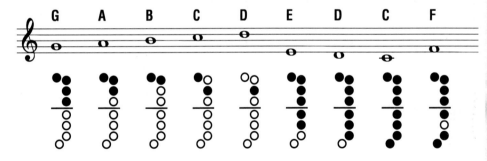

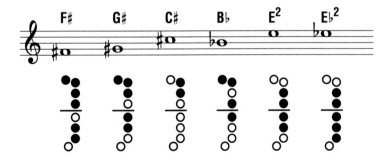

Recorders come in many sizes; the larger ones sound lower, and the smaller ones sound higher.

An alto recorder is larger than a soprano recorder. It uses the same set of fingerings but produces different pitches.

Play these pitches on a soprano recorder.

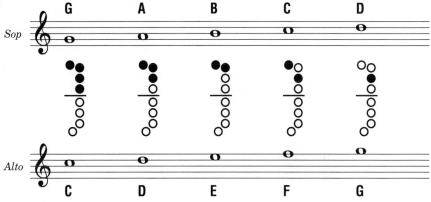

Use the same fingering on an alto recorder. Notice that the pitches are different. Now play these new pitches on an alto.

Play the melody from "Hineh Mah Tov." This is Part I of the round and can be played as an ostinato.

Here is an alto countermelody for "When the Saints Go Marching In."

Try a countermelody to "The Cowpoke."

Playing the Autoharp

How to Hold the Autoharp

Hold the autoharp with the small end in front of your left shoulder and the large end resting on your left leg. Wrap your left arm around the autoharp, well below the pegs. Make sure you can press all the chord bars comfortably with your right hand.

Let your right elbow rest lightly on the front corner of the autoharp. When you strum the strings, do not move your upper arm. Let your wrist bend as you move your right arm freely over all the strings, close to the chord bars.

The girl in the photograph is holding the autoharp in this way, called folk style. This position gives you the freedom to develop right-hand accompaniments without crossing your arms.

Check your playing position in a mirror. Work toward varying the volume and achieving control. Experiment—it takes time to be comfortable.

How to Wear the Picks

Using picks provides greater volume and pitch control. Picks also help prevent damage to your fingertips. Most music stores sell plastic picks and metal picks.

You will need a thumb pick. It should fit snugly, covering most of your thumbnail.

You will also need one metal fingerpick with a gauge number between 15 and 25 (the higher the gauge number, the stiffer the metal). Put the pick on your middle finger and push it down snugly so that it protrudes only about a quarter inch past the tip of your finger.

Easy Thumb-Strum Accompaniments

The strum patterns shown below provide good accompaniment patterns for the songs in your book. Strum on each beat with your right thumb, making a long stroke when the arrow is long and a short stroke when it is short.

Duple-Meter Thumb Strums

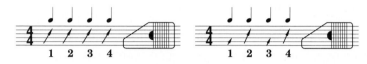

When you have mastered these strums, use them to accompany "Are You Sleeping?" on page 103. This song uses only one chord.

> Here are more songs in duple meter that you can play.
> - Give a Little Love, page 18
> - Hold 'em, Joe, page 86
> - Jamaica Farewell, page 12
> - When the Saints Go Marching In, page 277

Triple-Meter Thumb Strums

> Try these songs in triple meter.
> - El capotín, page 104
> - Las mañanitas, page 110
> - The Cowpoke, page 117
> - We Wish You a Merry Christmas, page 213

Left-Hand Finger Patterns

Most autoharp players use the index, middle, and ring fingers for playing three-chord melodies. Choose a different finger for each chord. Rest each finger lightly atop its chord bar throughout the song.

Fingerpicking Accompaniments

The middle-finger stroke always starts at or near the high strings and moves toward the low strings.

As you begin to use your middle finger, think of your right arm as a pendulum that swings steadily back and forth over the strings. When it swings from low to high, your thumb strikes the strings. When it swings from high to low, your middle finger strikes the strings.

Count out loud as you play, saying, "One and two and three and four and..." Your thumb plays as you say each number. Your middle finger plays when you say each *and*.

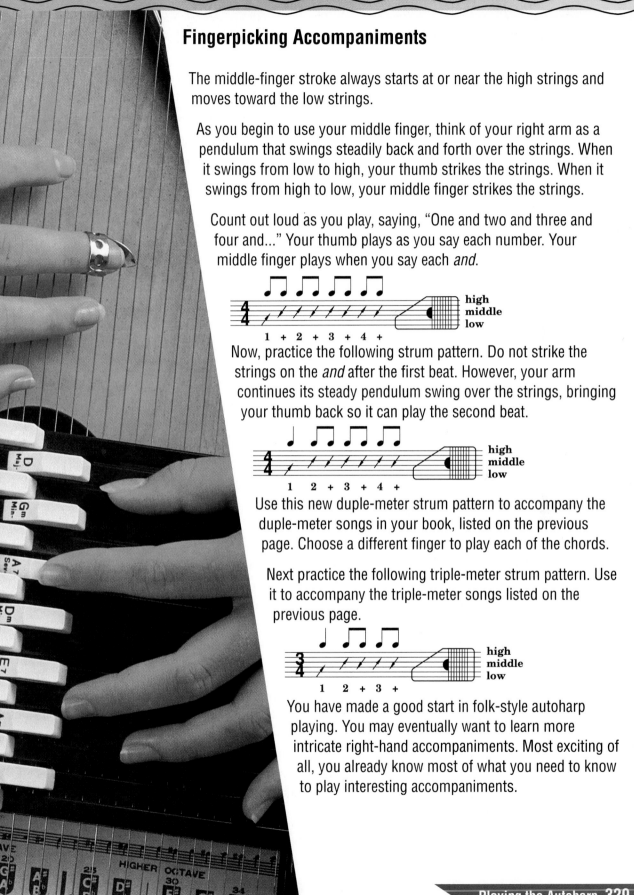

Now, practice the following strum pattern. Do not strike the strings on the *and* after the first beat. However, your arm continues its steady pendulum swing over the strings, bringing your thumb back so it can play the second beat.

Use this new duple-meter strum pattern to accompany the duple-meter songs in your book, listed on the previous page. Choose a different finger to play each of the chords.

Next practice the following triple-meter strum pattern. Use it to accompany the triple-meter songs listed on the previous page.

You have made a good start in folk-style autoharp playing. You may eventually want to learn more intricate right-hand accompaniments. Most exciting of all, you already know most of what you need to know to play interesting accompaniments.

Sound Bank

BASS DRUM   A large cylinder-shaped drum. The player can beat one or both sides with a large beater.

The bass drum has a low, booming sound, which can be soft and fuzzy or loud and demanding. (p. 56)

BASSOON   A large tube-shaped woodwind instrument with a double reed. A long, curved stem joins the tube and the mouthpiece. The player blows into the reed to make the sound and presses keys to change the pitch.

Lower notes on the bassoon may sound gruff or comical. Higher pitches sound softer and more gentle. (p. 53)

BERIMBAU (beh reem BAU) *See* UGHUBU.

CELLO   (CHEH loh) A large wooden string instrument. The player sits with the cello between his or her knees and reaches around the front to play. The cello may be plucked with the fingers or played with a bow.

The cello has a rich, warm voice that can sound quite low. However, some of the cello's best notes are in the middle register. (p. 59)

CHARANGO   (chah RAHN goh) A small guitar that has five double sets of strings. It may have a round back (made either from the shell of an armadillo or from carved wood) or a flat back (made of cedar or walnut). The strings are strummed or plucked with the fingernails.

The charango is often used in Peruvian and Bolivian music. It has a sharp, high-pitched sound. (p. 100)

CLARINET   A cylinder-shaped wind instrument with a reed in the mouthpiece. It is usually made of wood but may be plastic or metal. The player blows into the mouthpiece and presses keys to change the pitch.

The lower notes of the clarinet are soft and hollow. The middle notes are open and bright, and the notes in the upper register are thinner and more piercing. (p. 53)

CUATRO (KWAH troh) *See* TIPLE.

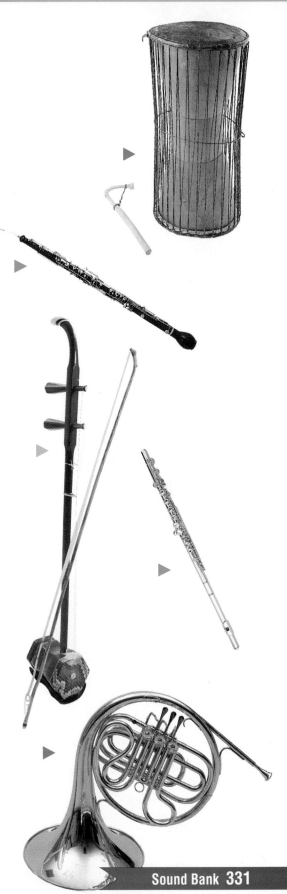

DUNDUN DRUM (doon DOON) West African double-headed drums. Most dundun drums have an hourglass shape. The ends are covered with goatskin drumheads that are fastened together with thongs or cords stretched down the length of the drum. Pressing the cords tightens the drumheads, producing sharp, high sounds.

Dundun drums are known as talking or singing drums because they can match the pitch and rhythm of spoken language. (p. 222)

ENGLISH HORN A long wooden cylinder-shaped wind instrument with a double reed. There is a bulb-shaped bell at one end of the instrument. Pitch is changed by pressing keys.

The sound of the English horn is similar to that of the oboe. However, the English horn has a lower, warmer range of notes. (p. 53)

ERHU (ehr hoo) A Chinese string instrument with a long round hardwood neck that has two tuning pegs at the upper end. The lower end is inserted into a resonator. The instrument has two steel strings and is played with a horsehair bow that is supported by a bamboo stem.

The erhu sounds something like a violin. It is an important instrument in modern Chinese orchestras. It is also popular as a solo instrument for recitals. (p. 108)

FLUTE A small metal instrument shaped like a pipe. The player holds the instrument sideways and blows across the open mouthpiece to make a sound. Pitch is changed by pressing keys and fingering holes on the side of the instrument.

The flute has a high voice, with a clear, sweet sound. (p. 52)

FRENCH HORN A medium-sized instrument made of coiled brass tubing. It has a large bell at one end and a funnel-shaped mouthpiece at the other. The player holds the horn in his or her lap, with one hand inside the bell. Valves on the side of the horn are pressed to change pitch.

The sound of the French horn is mellow and warm. (p. 54)

GUITAR (acoustic) A wooden instrument with six strings. The player strums or plucks the strings with a pick or the fingers to play a melody or chords.

When played softly, the guitar sounds gentle and sweet. It sounds lush and powerful when it is played more loudly. (p. 110)

GUITAR (electric) Electric guitars are flatter than acoustic guitars and are usually made of wood. They must be plugged into an amplifier.

Electric guitars are much louder than acoustic guitars. They can make many special sounds with the help of electronics. (p. 238)

HARP A large instrument with strings stretched vertically in an open, triangular frame. The player plucks the strings and operates foot pedals to play chromatic tones.

Present-day harps can play 6 1/2 octaves. Rippling chords are characteristic sounds of the instrument. (p. 266)

MBIRA (m BEE rah) An African finger xylophone made of 5 to 30 or more thin metal or cane tongues attached to a sounding board. The tongues are plucked with the thumbs and forefingers. The length of each tongue determines its pitch. The sound may be amplified with a gourd. The mbira has been exported to Latin America. Other names for it are sansa and thumb piano.

Each tongue of the mbira produces a soft sound when struck, similar to that of a xylophone. Rattles are sometimes attached to the tongues. (p. 222)

OBOE A small wooden cylinder-shaped wind instrument. The player blows into a double reed and changes pitch by pressing keys and fingering holes on the side of the instrument.

The sound of the oboe is thin, sweet, and often exotic. The higher notes are softer, the lower notes are more harsh and edgy. (p. 52)

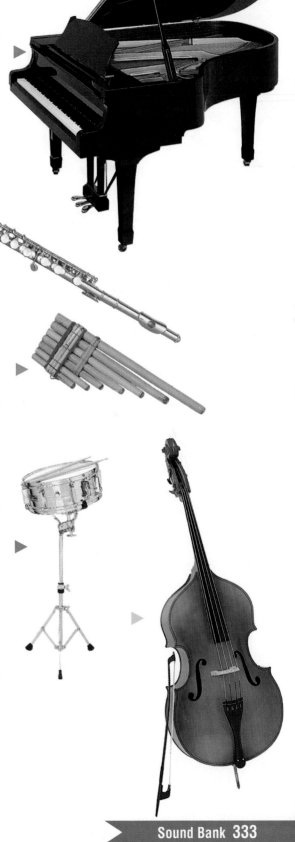

PIANO A large keyboard instrument capable of playing 88 different keys, or pitches. When the player presses the keys, hammers inside the piano strike strings to produce the sound. The strings are attached to a soundboard, which amplifies the sound.

The piano can play high and low notes. Many notes can be sounded at the same time. (p. 88)

PICCOLO A very small flute.

The piccolo's sound is like that of the flute's but higher and more piercing. (p. 52)

SANSA (SAHN sah) *See* MBIRA.

SIKU (SEE koo) A South Andean panpipe. This wind instrument consists of one or more rows of pipes, or tubes, of graduated lengths bound together and played by blowing across the open upper ends. Sikus come in a variety of sizes.

Each pipe of a siku has its own pitch. The longer the pipe, the lower its pitch. Sikus are played at dances and fiestas as well as in orchestras. They are often accompanied by drums. (p. 27)

SNARE DRUM A small cylinder-shaped drum with two heads. Snares, or strings wrapped with wire, are stretched across the bottom head to create a vibrating sound.

A snare drum can make a long, raspy roll or a sharp, rhythmic, beating sound. (p. 56)

STRING BASS This largest of the string instruments is so tall that a player must sit on a high stool or stand up to play it. The player reaches around the front of the string bass to pluck it or bow it.

The voice of the string bass is deep, dark, and sometimes rumbling. (p. 59)

THUMB PIANO *See* MBIRA.

TIMPANI Large basin-shaped drums made of copper or brass, also called kettledrums. The timpani can be tuned to specific pitches, and the player often uses several drums to play melodic patterns.

The timpani can create dramatic effects, sounding like crashing thunder, a quiet heartbeat, or marching feet. (p. 57)

TIPLE (TEE pleh) A small guitar. The Colombian tiple has four sets of three steel strings. The strings in the first set are identical; the other three sets each contain two identical strings and a third string that sounds an octave lower.

The tiple's special grouping of strings gives Caribbean music its distinctive sound. The Colombian tiple resembles the Cuban tres and the Puerto Rican cuatro. (p. 95)

TRES *See* TIPLE.

TROMBONE A large brass instrument with a bell at one end of the tubing. Pitch is changed by moving a long slide on the side of the instrument.

One of the loudest instruments in a Western orchestra, the trombone may sound very noisy and aggressive. It can also sound very warm and mellow. (p. 55)

TRUMPET A small brass instrument with a bell at one end of its coiled tubing. The player pushes three button-shaped valves at the top of the instrument to change pitch.

The sound of the trumpet is bold and bright. Playing a lyrical melody it can sound sweet, even sad. (p. 55)

TUBA   The largest brass instrument, with a very large bell that usually points upward. The player changes the pitch by pressing valves.

The tuba's sound is very low, deep, and sturdy. When playing a melody, it can sound surprisingly rich and mellow. (p. 55)

UGHUBU   (oog HOO boo)   A large musical bow with a gourd resonator attached. The open end of the gourd is held against the body as the single string made of twisted cow-tail hair is struck with a stick, a thin reed, or a piece of straw. Zulu people of southern Africa often play the ughubu to accompany their singing as they travel. In Brazil this type of musical bow is called a berimbau.

The ughubu basically has two pitches. By moving the gourd resonator, overtones can be created. (p. 222)

VIOLA   (vee OH lah) A wooden string instrument that is slightly larger than the violin. The viola is held under the player's chin and either bowed or plucked.

The viola's tone is deeper and more mellow than the violin's, but very similar to it. (p. 58)

VIOLIN   The smallest string instrument in a Western orchestra. The violin can make a very large sound when plucked or bowed. It is held under the player's chin.

The violin can make many different sounds. Its tone can be brilliant, warm, raspy, shrill, vibrant, harsh, or mellow. (p. 58)

ZHENG   (cheng) A Chinese type of plucked zither, with movable bridges. The sides and bottom of a zheng are usually made of hardwood. The soundboard is made of softer wood. The zheng usually has 16 strings.

When playing a zheng, the player uses the fingernails on the right hand to pluck the strings; the left hand is used to apply pressure to the strings. The sound is similar to that of a harp. (p. 108)

Glossary

accelerando (p. 174)   Making the tempo, or speed of music, get gradually faster.

accent (p. 20)   A single tone or chord louder than those around it (>).

accompaniment (p. 12)   Music that supports the sound of the featured performer(s).

antiphonal (p. 90)   "Sound against sound," or one group echoing or answering another.

band (p. 144)   A balanced group of instruments, consisting of woodwinds, brass, and percussion.

beat (p. 8)   A repeating pulse that can be felt in some music.

cadence (p. 26)   A group of chords or notes at the end of a phrase or piece that give a feeling of pausing or finishing.

call and response (p. 84)   A follow-the-leader process in which a melody is introduced by one voice or instrument and then immediately answered by other voices or instruments.

canon (p. 38)   A form in which a melody begins in one part and then is imitated by other parts in an overlapping manner.

choir (p. 55)   Commonly used to mean a group of singers performing together. Also a group of instruments, as in a brass *choir*.

chord (p. 114)   Three or more different tones played or sung together.

chord progression (p. 115)   The order of chords in a segment of a piece of music.

chromatic scale (p. 102)   A consecutive succession of twelve tones, each a half step apart.

composer (p. 33)   A person who makes up pieces of music by putting sounds together in his or her own way.

concerto (p. 140)   A piece for a solo instrument with orchestra, usually in three movements.

contour (p. 28)   The "shape" of a melody, made by the way it moves upward and downward in steps and leaps, and by repeated tones.

contrast (p. 30)   Two or more things that are different. In music, for example, slow is a *contrast* to fast; Section A is a *contrast* to Section B.

countermelody (p. 13)   A melody that is played or sung at the same time as another melody.

duet (p. 110)   Any two-part composition written for two performers.

ensemble (p. 155)   A group of players or singers.

fanfare (p. 55)   A tune for one or more brass instruments; it is usually short and made of strong, accented passages. Fanfares are often used to announce someone or something.

form (p. 60)   The structure of a composition; the way its musical materials are organized.

harmony (p. 13)   Two or more different tones sounding at the same time.

interval (p. 102)   The distance between tones.

jazz (p. 133)   An American musical style made of traditional Western music combined with African rhythms and melodic contours.

leap (p. 25)   To move from one tone to another, skipping over the tones in between.

lyrics (p. 29)   The words of a song.

major scale (p. 102)   An arrangement of eight tones in a scale according to the following steps: whole, whole, half, whole, whole, whole, half.

medium (p. 46)   The materials used in creating a work of art much like the instruments used in writing a piece of music.

melody (p. 12)   A line of single tones that move upward, downward, or repeat.

meter (p. 10)   The way beats of music are grouped, often in sets of two or in sets of three.

minor scale (p. 103)   Any of several arrangements of eight tones in a scale, such as natural minor: whole, half, whole, whole, half, whole, whole.

mood (p. 43)   The feeling that a piece of music gives. The *mood* of a lullaby is quiet and gentle.

opera (p. 168)   A musical play in which most of the speaking lines are sung.

operetta (p. 168)   A musical play, often similar to an opera but usually less serious. In an operetta most of the dialogue is spoken.

orchestra (p. 50)   A performing group of various instruments. The term can be applied to many different ensembles, such as the Western symphony orchestra or the Japanese *gagaku* orchestra (p. 107).

ostinato (p. 21)   A rhythm or melody pattern that repeats.

overture (p. 75)   A piece of music originally designed to be played before the beginning of an opera or musical play, often containing melodies that will be heard later in the work.

parody (p. 264)   A humorous imitation.

pentatonic (p. 106)   Music based on a five-tone scale. A common pentatonic scale corresponds to tones 1, 2, 3, 5, and 6 of the major scale.

phrase (p. 26)   A musical sentence. Each phrase expresses a thought.

pitch (p. 24)   The location of a tone with respect to highness or lowness.

quodlibet (p. 262)   Literally, "debate." A composition made up of several melodies sounded in succession or at the same time.

range (p. 42)   In a melody, the span from the lowest tone to the highest tone.

rondo (p. 66)   A musical form in which the main musical idea, A, is repeated, with contrasting sections in between (ABACA).

round (p. 40)   A follow-the-leader process in which all voices sing the same melody but start at different times. A round is a kind of canon, but a round is usually repeated (with each voice starting over) a number of times.

scale (p. 102)   An arrangement of pitches from lower to higher, according to a specific pattern of intervals.

score (p. 52)   Written music or notation of a composition, with each of the vocal or instrumental parts appearing in vertical alignment.

sequence (p. 30)   The repetition of a melody pattern at a higher or lower pitch level.

step (p. 25)   To move from one tone to another, upward or downward, without skipping scale tones in between.

symphony (p. 52)   A large, usually lengthy, piece of art music for a full Western orchestra. The term is also sometimes used to mean "symphony orchestra."

syncopation (p. 92)   An arrangement of rhythm in which prominent or important tones begin on weak beats or weak parts of beats, giving a catchy, off-balance movement to the music.

tempo (p. 16)   The speed of the beat.

theme (p. 32)   An important melody that occurs several times in a piece of music.

theme and variations (p. 68)   A composition, each section of which is an alteration of the initial theme.

tonal center (p. 26)   The key a piece of music is in. Often the tonal center will be the first or last note of a piece.

tone color (p. 42)   The unique sound of an instrument or voice.

unison (p. 32)   The same pitch.

whole tone scale (p. 109)   A consecutive succession of six tones, each a whole step apart.

Classified Index

FOLK, TRADITIONAL, AND REGIONAL

Africa
See also Ghana, Senegal, South Africa.
Kum Ba Yah   280

African American
Abraham, Martin, and John   188
Didn't My Lord Deliver Daniel?   92
Do, Lord   99
Ezekiel Saw the Wheel   290
Free at Last   190
Hold the Wind   309
Joshua Fought the Battle of Jericho   294
Lean on Me   128
Little Wheel A-Turnin'   42
Long John   84
Michael, Row the Boat Ashore   88
Now Let Me Fly   80
Peace like a River   82
Rock-a My Soul   273
Shake Hands, Mary   295
We Are the World   4
When the Saints Go Marching In   277

American Indian
See Native American.

Belgium
Snow-White Bird, A   292

Bolivia
Butterfly, The *(La mariposa)*   27
Traditional: *Qunapaquí (Why?)*   155

Canada
Carrion Crow (Nova Scotia)   298

Chile
Leavin' for Chile *(Cuando pa' Chile me voy)*   100
My White Horse *(Mi caballo blanco)*   15
Traditional: *Cuando pa' Chile me voy*   101

China
Boat on the Lake, A *(Tai-hu)*   108
Traditional: *Chunjiang huayueye*   155
Traditional: *Purple Bamboo Melody*   108

Cuba
León: *Indigena*   187
Rodriguez: *Tumba la caña*   95

England
Barb'ry Allen   261
Blow the Wind Southerly   269, 304
Fox, The   260
Good King Wenceslas   212
Greensleeves   271, 300
Holly and the Ivy, The   208
Miller of Dee, The   296
Nottamun Town   267
Now Is the Month of Maying   306
Scarborough Fair   70
Water Is Wide, The   286
We Wish You a Merry Christmas   213
Wraggle-Taggle Gypsies, The   263

France
Ding-Dong Merrily On High   204
Vive L'Amour   37

Germany
Gaudeamus igitur   74
Silent Night   203

Sing to the Lord *(Singt dem Herren)* 41
Stately House, The *(Wir hatten gebauet)* 75
What Comes There O'er the Hill? *(Was kommt dort von der Höh?)* 74

Ghana
See also Africa.
Traditional: *Kelo aba w'ye* 157

Hispanic American
Eres tú *(Touch the Wind)* 181

Hungary
Farmer Jacob 257

Indonesia
Suliram 289

Israel, Hebrew, Jewish
Around About Chanukah 201
Dona Dona 174
Hava Nagila 158
Hineh Mah Tov *(How Good the Time)* 279
O Chanukah 200
Traditional: *Mayim! Mayim!* (Israel) 158
Yibane Amenu 40

Italy
Band from Assori, The *(Il tamburo della banda d'Assori)* 150

Jamaica
Jamaica Farewell 12
Marley: *One Love* 16

Japan.
See also Okinawa.
Traditional: *Entenraku* 107

Latin America
Cantaré, cantarás *(I Will Sing, You Will Sing)* 226
Hammond and Calderón: *Cantaré, cantarás* 227

Mexico
Así es mi tierra 214
Cowpoke, The *(El payo)* 117
Las mañanitas 110
Springtime *(La primavera)* 112
Traditional: *La leva* 144

Native American
Go, My Son 120
Traditional: *Round Dance Song* (Taos Indian) 123

Okinawa
See also Japan.
Asadoya 106

Polynesia
Traditional: *Samoan Coconut* 157

Puerto Rico
El capotín 104
Head for the Canefields *(Corta la caña)* 94

Russia
Minka 291
Traditional: *Troika* 157

Scotland
Auld Lang Syne 279
Charlie Is My Darling 297
Farewell to Tarwathie 258
Great Silkie, The 311
Little Boy of the Sheep 270

Senegal
See also Africa.
Traditional: *Senegalese Drumming*   155

South Africa
See also Africa.
Siyahamba (Zulu)   222

Spain
Rodrigo: *Fantasia para un gentilhombre,* "Torch
   Dance"   89

United States
See also African American, Hispanic American, Native
   American, Puerto Rico.
America   195
America, the Beautiful   194
Blow, Ye Winds   285
Charlottetown   173
Come, Ye Thankful People, Come   199
Deep in the Heart of Texas   282
Down the Ohio   36
Every Night When the Sun Goes In   310
Home on the Range   281
I Wonder as I Wander   278
Love Somebody   274
New River Train   283
Old Dan Tucker   284
Old Joe Clark   312
Old Texas   272, 275
One Morning in May   265
Springfield Mountain   272, 275
Star-Spangled Banner, The   192
Yonder Stands a Handsome Lady   305

Venezuela
Song of the Water *(Canto del agua)*   124

Vietnam
Wind on the Bridge, The *(Quâ Câu Gió Bay)*   126

West Indies
Give a Little Love   18
Hold 'em, Joe   86

HOLIDAY, SEASONAL, AND SPECIAL
OCCASION

Birthday
Las mañanitas   110

December
Around About Chanukah   201
Auld Lang Syne   279
Christmas Is a Time for Sharing   206
Ding-Dong Merrily On High   204
Gloria, Gloria   202
Good King Wenceslas   212
Holly and the Ivy, The   208
I Wonder As I Wander   278
O Chanukah   200
Silent Night   203
We Wish You a Merry Christmas   213

Martin Luther King, Jr. Day
Abraham, Martin, and John   188
Answer Lies in You and in Me, The   96
Free at Last   190
I Am But a Small Voice   196

Patriotic

Abraham, Martin, and John   188
America   195
America, the Beautiful   194
I Am But a Small Voice   196
Star-Spangled Banner, The   192

Spring

Así es mi tierra   214
Now Is the Month of Maying   306
One Morning in May   265
Springtime *(La primavera)*   112

Thanksgiving

Come, Ye Thankful People, Come   199

United Nations Day

Answer Lies in You and in Me, The   96
Cantaré, cantarás (*I Will Sing, You Will Sing*)   226
I Am But a Small Voice   196
Love in Any Language   216
Sing a Song of Peace   220
Siyahamba   222
United Nations, The   229
We Are the World   4

LISTENING SELECTIONS

Anonymous: *Greensleeves to a Ground*   300

Bach, J.S.: *Jesu, Joy of Man's Desiring*   28
Bach, J.S.: *Sonata in G Minor for Unaccompanied Violin,* "Presto"   85
Bach, P.D.Q.: *Birthday Ode to "Big Daddy" Bach, S. 100*   23

Bates/Ward: *America, the Beautiful* (gospel version)   194
Beethoven: *Für Elise*   66
Beethoven: *Symphony No. 9 in D Minor,* "March" (percussion exc.)   57
Beethoven: *Symphony No. 9 in D Minor,* "Scherzo" (timpani exc.)   57
Berlioz: *Roman Carnival Overture*   50
Bernstein: *Candide,* "Overture"   49
Bernstein: *West Side Story,* "America"   21
Borodin: *Polovtsian Dance No. 2* (oboe exc.)   52
Brahms: *Academic Festival Overture*   76
Britten: *A Ceremony of Carols,* "Balulalow"   21
Britten: *Young Person's Guide to the Orchestra* (violin exc.)   58
Burgie: *Jamaica Farewell*   13

Copland: *Appalachian Spring,* "Variations on 'Simple Gifts'"   180

Desmond: *Take Five*   61
di Lasso: *Echo Song* (brass)   55
di Lasso: *Echo Song* (vocal)   90
Dukas: *La péri,* "Overture"   144
Dukas: *Sorcerer's Apprentice* (bassoon exc.)   53
Dvořák: *Symphony No. 9,* Mvt. 2 (English horn exc.)   53
Dvořák: *Slavonic Dance No. 8 in G Minor, Op. 46*   105

Earth Tribe Rhythms: *Caribbean Sea*   11
Ehrlich: *Take Me To the World*   6

Gershwin: *An American In Paris*   133
Gershwin: *Concerto in F,* Mvt. 3   141
Gershwin: *I Got Rhythm*   143

Gershwin: *Rhapsody in Blue*   133
Gray: *A String of Pearls*   154

Hamlisch: *A Chorus Line*, "One"   169
Hammond and Calderón: *Cantaré, cantarás*   227
Handel: *Water Music Suite*, "Allegro"   90
Haydn: *Symphony No. 94*, Mvt. 2   308
Holst: *Suite for Band*, "Fantasia on Dargason" 153
Holst: *The Planets*, "Jupiter"   59

Ives: *Variations on "America"*   68

Joel: *Root Beer Rag*   134
Joel: *The Ballad of Billy the Kid*   185
Joel: *We Didn't Start the Fire*   185
Joplin: *Pineapple Rag*   134

Khachaturian: *Masquerade Suite*, "Waltz"   14

León: *Indigena*   187
Lloyd Webber: *Cats*, "Mr. Mistoffelees"   169
Lloyd Webber: *Requiem*, "Pie Jesu"   110

MacGregor: *Intrusion of the Hunter*   57
Mahler: *Symphony No. 1 in D Major*, Mvt. 3   39
Marley: *One Love*   16
Milhaud: *Saudades do Brasil*, "Laranjeiras"   61
Miller: *In the Mood*   154
Mozart: *Eine kleine Nachtmusik*, "Minuet"   85
Mozart: *Sonata in A Major*, Mvt. 1   270
Mussorgsky: *Pictures at an Exhibition*, "Bydlo" (tuba exc.)   55
Mussorgsky: *Pictures at an Exhibition*, "Bydlo"   49
Mussorgsky: *Pictures at an Exhibition*, "Great Gate of Kiev" (chimes exc.)   57

Nelson, Willie: *On the Road Again*   33

Orff: *Carmina Burana*, "Tanz"   21

Prokofiev: *Lieutenant Kijé Suite*, Mvt. 1 (piccolo exc.)   52
Prokofiev: *Lieutenant Kijé Suite*, "Romance" (string bass exc.)   58
Prokofiev: *Peter and the Wolf, Op. 67* (clarinet exc.)   53
Prokofiev: *Symphony No. 1 in D*, "Gavotte"   28
Purcell: *Sonata in D for Trumpet and Strings*, Mvt. 1   89

Rachmaninoff: *Piano Concerto No. 2 in C Minor*, Mvt. 3 (viola exc.)   58
Ravel: *Daphnis and Chloe Suite* (flute exc.)   52
Ravel: *Le Tombeau de Couperin*, "Minuet" (orchestra exc.)   47
Ravel: *Le Tombeau de Couperin*, "Minuet" (piano exc.)   47
Red: *Woodwind Fantasy on a Thanksgiving Song*   53
Rodrigo: *Fantasia para un gentilhombre*, "Torch Dance"   89
Rodriguez: *Tumba la caña*   95

Saint-Saëns: *Carnival of the Animals*, "Fossils" (xylophone exc.)   56
Smetana: *Ma Vlast*, "The Moldau"   266
Smith/Bernard: *Winter Wonderland*   210
Sousa: *Semper Fidelis*   145
Strauss: *Till Eulenspiegel's Merry Pranks* (French horn exc.)   54
Stravinsky: *Petrouchka*, Themes from Scene IV   166

Tchaikovsky: *Symphony No. 5 in E Minor*, Mvt. 2 (cello exc.)   58
Traditional Bolivian: *Qunapaqui (Why?)*   155
Traditional Chilean: *Cuando pa' Chile me voy*   101
Traditional Chinese: *Chunjiang huayueye*   155
Traditional Chinese: *Purple Bamboo Melody*   108
Traditional English: *Good King Wenceslas*   212
Traditional Ghanian: *Kelo aba w'ye*   157
Traditional Israeli: *Mayim! Mayim!*   158
Traditional Japanese: *Entenraku*   107
Traditional Mexican: *La leva*   144
Traditional Polynesian: *Samoan Coconut*   157
Traditional Russian: *Troika*   157
Traditional Senegalese: *Senegalese Drumming* 155
Traditional Taos Indian: *Round Dance Song*   123
Traditional: *Are You Sleeping?* (major)   103
Traditional: *Are You Sleeping?* (minor)   103
Traditional: *Are You Sleeping?* (pentatonic)   108
Traditional: *Are You Sleeping?* (whole tone)   109
Traditional: *Scarborough Fair* (7 variations)   71

Verdi: *Aida*, "Grand March" (trumpet exc.)   55

Wagner: *Tannhäuser*, "Pilgrims' Chorus" (trombone exc.)   55
Williams, L.: *Battery* (snare drum/bass drum, cymbals exc.)   56
Willson: *The Music Man*, "Seventy-Six Trombones"   168

Withers: *Lean on Me*   129

Zaimont: *A Calendar Set*, "December"   118
Zaimont: *Reflective Rag*   134

PERFORMANCE MUSICAL: "IT'S A FAM'LY"

I Need Help!   232
It's a Fam'ly   250
My Life   238
Pass the Ball   244
Prologue   231
There's a Boy I Dream Of   246

POETRY AND TRADEBOOK SELECTIONS

Barter   197
Encouragement II   189
Way to Start a Day, The   66

RECORDED INTERVIEWS

Careers in Music
Billy Joel   184, 185
Tania León   187

THEME MUSICAL: UNITED NATIONS DAY

Cantaré, cantarás (*I Will Sing, You Will Sing*)   226
Sing a Song of Peace   220
Siyahamba   222
United Nations, The   229

$\mathcal{S}$ong $\mathcal{I}$ndex CD-Track Number

Abraham, Martin, and John 188   8-2
Alexander's Ragtime Band 135   5-27
Alphabet, The 314   11-15
America 195   8-10
America, the Beautiful 194   8-7
Annie Lee 25   1-21
Answer Lies in You and in Me, The 96   4-16
Around About Chanukah 201   8-16
Asadoya 106   4-29
Así es mi tierra 214   8-27
Auld Lang Syne 279   10-22

Band from Assori, The *(Il tamburo della banda d'Assori)* 150   6-10
Barb'ry Allen 261   10-2
Blow the Wind Southerly 269, 304   10-11
Blow, Ye Winds 285   10-29
Boat on the Lake, A *(Tai-hu)* 108   4-31
Butterfly, The *(La mariposa)* 27   1-22
Bye-Bye, Blues 171   7-11

Cantaré, cantarás *(I Will Sing, You Will Sing)* 226   9-4
Canto del agua *(Song of the Water)* 124   5-17
Carrion Crow 298   11-4
Catch a Falling Star 38   2-7
Charleston 165   7-6
Charlie Is My Darling 297   11-3
Charlottetown 173   7-12
Christmas Is a Time for Sharing 206   8-20
Come Follow the Band 146   6-9
Come, Ye Thankful People, Come 199   8-14
Corta la caña *(Head for the Canefields)* 94   4-13
Country Style 160   7-4
Cowpoke, The *(El payo)* 117   5-10
Cuando pa' Chile me voy *(Leavin' for Chile)* 100   4-21

Deep in the Heart of Texas 282   10-26
Didn't My Lord Deliver Daniel? 92   4-12
Ding-Dong Merrily On High 204   8-19
Do, Lord 99   4-18
Dona Dona 174   7-13
Down the Ohio 36   2-4

El capotín 104   4-26, 27
El payo *(The Cowpoke)* 117   5-11

Eres tú *(Touch the Wind)* 181   7-16
Every Night When the Sun Goes In 310   11-12
Ezekiel Saw the Wheel 290   10-33

Farewell to Tarwathie 259   9-27
Farmer Jacob 257   9-26
Fox, The 260   10-1
Free at Last 190   8-5

Gaudeamus igitur 74   3-18
Give a Little Love 18   1-13
Gloria, Gloria 202   8-17
Go, My Son 120   5-13
Good King Wenceslas 212   8-24
Grasshoppers Three 302   11-6
Great Silkie, The 311   11-13
Greensleeves 271, 300   10-14

Hava Nagila 158   7-1
Head for the Canefields *(Corta la caña)* 94   4-13
Hineh Mah Tov *(How Good the Time)* 279   10-21
Hold 'em, Joe 86   4-5
Hold the Wind 309   11-11
Holly and the Ivy, The 208   8-22
Home on the Range 281   10-25
How Good the Time *(Hineh Mah Tov)* 279   10-21

I Am But a Small Voice 196   8-11
I Got Rhythm 143   6-3
I Need Help! 232   9-12
I Will Sing, You Will Sing *(Cantaré, cantarás)* 226   9-4
I Wonder as I Wander 278   10-20
Il tamburo della banda d'Assori *(The Band from Assori)* 150   6-11
It's a Fam'ly 250   9-16
It's a Good Day 64   3-5

Jamaica Farewell 12   1-7
Joshua Fought the Battle of Jericho 294   10-36

Kum Ba Yah 280   10-23

La mariposa (*The Butterfly*) 27   1-23
La primavera (*Springtime*) 112   5-9
Las mañanitas 110   5-5
Latin America (chant) 20   1-15
Lean on Me 128   5-19
Leatherwing Bat 256   9-25
Leavin' for Chile (*Cuando pa' Chile me voy*) 100   4-20
Little Boy of the Sheep 270   10-12
Little Tom Tinker 264   10-5
Little Wheel A-Turnin' 42   2-12
Long John 84   4-2
Love in Any Language 216   8-29
Love Somebody 274   10-18

Mi caballo blanco (*My White Horse*) 15   1-11
Michael, Row the Boat Ashore 88   4-6
Miller of Dee, The 296   11-2
Minka 291   10-34
Music Goes with Anything 43   2-13
My Life 238   9-13
My White Horse (*Mi caballo blanco*) 15   1-10

New River Train 283   10-27
No-Name Bossa Nova 63   3-4
Nottamun Town 267   10-10
Now Is the Month of Maying 306   11-8
Now Let Me Fly 80   3-25

O Chanukah 200   8-15
Old Dan Tucker 284   10-28
Old Joe Clark 312   11-14
Old Texas 272, 275   10-15
On the Road Again 32   1-27
One Morning in May 265   10-7

Pass the Ball 243   9-14
Peace like a River 82   3-27
Prologue (*from "It's a Fam'ly"*) 231   9-11
Put on a Happy Face 8   1-4

Quâ Câu Gió Bay (*The Wind on the Bridge*) 126   5-18

Rock-a My Soul 273   10-17

Scarborough Fair 70   3-9
Shake Hands, Mary 295   11-1
Sheep May Safely Graze 176   7-14
Silent Night 203   8-18
Sing a Song of Peace 220   9-1
Sing to the Lord (*Singt dem Herren*) 41   2-10
Singt dem Herren (*Sing to the Lord*) 41   2-10
Siyahamba 222   9-2, 3
Skye Boat Song 266   10-8
Snow-White Bird, A 292   10-35
Song of the Water (*Canto del agua*) 124   5-16
Springfield Mountain 272, 275   10-16
Springtime (*La primavera*) 112   5-9
Star-Spangled Banner, The 192   8-6
Stately House, The (*Wir hatten gebauet*) 75   3-22
Suliram 289   10-31
Swanee 138   5-29

Tai-hu (*A Boat on the Lake*) 108   4-31
Tea for Two 31   1-26
There's a Boy I Dream Of 246   9-15
Top of the World 34   2-2
Touch the Wind (*Eres tú*) 181   7-17

United Nations, The 229   9-6

Vive L'Amour 37   2-5

Was kommt dort von der Höh'? (*What Comes There O'er the Hill?*) 74   3-20
Water Is Wide, The 286   10-30
We Are the World 4   1-1
We Wish You a Merry Christmas 213   8-26
Welcome, Welcome, Every Guest 262   10-3
What Comes There O'er the Hill? (*Was kommt dort von der Höh'?*) 74   3-20
When the Saints Go Marching In 277   10-19
Wind on the Bridge, The (*Quâ Câu Gió Bay*) 126   5-18
Wir hatten gebauet (*The Stately House*) 75   3-22
Wraggle-Taggle Gypsies, The 263   10-4

Yibane Amenu 40   2-9
Yonder Stands a Handsome Lady 305   11-7

Acknowledgments

Credit and appreciation are due publishers and copyright owners for use of the following materials.

Cover: Music— © 1992 Jon Ehrlich and Robin Pogrebin

"Barter" by Sara Teasdale, from ANTHOLOGY OF CHILDREN'S LITERATURE. Houghton-Mifflin, 1959, acknowledged to Macmillan.

"Encouragement II" by John Henrik Clarke, from THE EARLY POEMS OF JOHN HENRIK CLARKE; Africa World Press. Originally published by Decker Press, 1948. First Africa World Edition 1991. "Take Me to the World" by Jon Erhlich and Robin Pogrebin, © 1992. "The Way to Start a Day" by Byrd Baylor; illustrated by Peter Parnall. Reprinted with permission of Charles Scribner's Sons, an imprint of Macmillan Company. Text © 1977, 1976 Byrd Baylor. Illustrations © 1978 Peter Parnall.

The editors of THE MUSIC CONNECTION have attempted to verify the sources of "The Band from Assori" (page 150), "Charlottetown" (page 173), and "Yonder Stands a Handsome Lady" (page 305). We believe them to be in the public domain.

Every effort has been made to locate all copyright holders of material used in this book. If any errors or omissions have occurred, corrections will be made.

Photograph and Illustration Credits

All photographs are by Silver Burdett Ginn (SBG) unless otherwise noted.

Cover: Mercedes McDonald.
2: Mary Thelen. 5: Harry Benson. 7: © 1995 M. & E. Bernheim/Woodfin Camp & Associates. 8: *l.* SuperStock, Inc.; *r.* Mike Busselle/Leo deWys, Inc. 9: *l.* © John G. Ross/Photo Researchers, Inc.; *m.* Rick Smolan/Leo deWys, Inc.; *r.* Steve Vidler/Leo deWys, Inc. 11: Paul Avis. 12–13: *ill.* Gerardo Suzan; *photo* Yoram Kahana/Shooting Star. 14: Doug Donne Bryant for SBG. 16–17: Bill James. 20–21: Springer/The Bettmann Archive. 24: *t.* Karl Gehring/LGI; *b.* R.J. Capak/London Features International. 26–27: Mary Haverfield. 28–29: *t. & border* Steve Vidler/Leo deWys, Inc.; *b.* Michael Busselle/Tony Stone Images, New York. 30–31: Paula Munck; *border* John Ceballos. 32–33: Blake Thornton. 34–35: NASA. 38–39: JoAnn Adinolfi. 40–41: Paula Munck. 42–45: JoAnn Adinolfi. 47: The Granger Collection. 48: Matisse, Henri. *Les Poissons Rouge,* 1912. Pushkin Museum, Moscow. © 1995, Succession H. Matisse/ARS, New York. Photograph: Scala/Art Resource. 50–51: *b.* Pam Hasegawa; *t.* The Granger Collection. 52–59: *photographs* Robert Daemmrich for SBG. 60–61: Jon Booth. 67: Peter Parnall. 68–69: The Bettmann Archive. 71–73: Joyce Patti. 74–79: Mary Haverfield. 76: *t.* Fridmar Damm/Leo deWys, Inc.; *b.* The Granger Collection. 77: Jan Morek. 80-81: Jennifer Hewittson. 83: *t.l.* LGI; *t.r.* Phil Loftus/London Features International; *m.t.* Alice Arnold/LGI; *m.r.* J. Bellissimo/LGI; *b.l.* Gary Merrin/London Features International; *b.r.* Clare Miller/LGI. 85: Martha Swope. 86–87: Jude Maceren. 89: The Bettmann Archive. 94–95: Raymond Ortiz Godfrey. 96–97: SuperStock. 98–99: *bkgd.* William Johnson/Stock, Boston; *electronically inset photo* Jon Riley/Tony Stone Images, New York. 104–105: Stephanie Langley. 106–107: *l.* Jean Paul Nacivet/Leo deWys Inc.; *r.* William Johnson/Stock, Boston. 108–109: *border ill.* James; *Hanging Scroll: Ni Tsan Woods and Valleys of Mount Yu.* Ink on paper. Yuan Dynasty (1279–1368), 1372. The Metropolitan Museum of Art, Gift of The Dillon Fund, 1973. (1973.120.8). 110–111: Kathleen Kinkopf. 112–113: Lee Rentz/Bruce Coleman, Inc. 114–115: Stuart Simons. 114: Steve Skjold for SBG. 116–117: Gerardo Suzan. 118–119: Karen Blessen. 120–121: *photograph* SuperStock; *border* Courtesy of Cotter Bay Indian Arts Museum, Grand Teton National Park, WY, photographed by Jerry Jacka. 122–123: Courtesy of Cotter Bay Indian Arts Museum, Grand Teton National Park, WY, photographed by Jerry Jacka; *insets* Elliot Smith for SBG. 124–125: *bkgd.* Russell Mittermeier/Bruce Coleman; *border* David J. Sams/Texas Inprint. 127: Phong Nguyen. 132–133: *border ill.* Karen Blessen. 132: *t.* Culver Pictures; *b.* Robert Daemmrich/Stock, Boston. 133: Culver Pictures. 134: Culver Pictures. 134–137: *ill.* Peggy Tagel. 135: The Granger Collection. 138–139: Roger Huyssen. 140–141: *ill.* JoAnn Adinolfi; *photograph* Crandall/The Image Works. 142–143: Roger

Huyssen. 144–145: *border ill.* Susan Todd; *photos* 144: Robert Daemmrich/.Stock, Boston. 145: *bkgd.* Jeff Hunter/The Image Bank; *inset* Culver Pictures. 146–149: *border ill.* Susan Todd; *photographs* SuperStock. 151: Michael Norcia/Leo deWys, Inc. 153: *bkgd.* Lucy Stone/Tony Stone Images, New York; *inset* The Bettmann Archive. 154–155: *ill.* Karen Blessen. 154: The Bettmann Archive. 155: From JVC Video Anthology of World Music and Dance, used by permission of Victor Company of Japan, Ltd. 156: *t.* Bingham, George Caleb. *The Jolly Flatboatman,* private collection on loan to National Gallery of Art, Washington, oil on canvas, .(969 x 1.232); *b.* The Bettmann Archive. 157: Joe Viesti/VIESTI ASSOCIATES, INC. 159: Richard Nowitz. 160–161: Gary Withey/Bruce Coleman. 162: Lynn Goldsmith. 163: *t., b.l.* Culver Pictures; *b.r.* Brown Brothers. 164: Culver Pictures. 166–167: Barbara Lambase. 168–169: *border ill.* Ken Spengler; *photos* Martha Swope. 170–171: *border ill.* Ron DuBuque; *photo* Travelpix/FPG INTERNATIONAL. 172–173: *border ill.* Karen Blessen; *photo* David Madison. 174–175: JoAnn Adinolfi. 176–177: Robert Daemmrich/Tony Stone Images, New York. 180–183: *border ill.* JoAnn Adinolfi. 180: UPI/The Bettmann Archive. 181: Robert Daemmrich for SBG. 184: Neal Preston/Maritime Music. 185: Jane Arginteanu/Maritime Music. 186–187: *border ill.* Ken Spengler. 188: *l.* The Bettmann Archive; *r.* Flip Schulke/Black Star. 189: *l.* Gene Daniels/Black Star; *r.* The Granger Collection. 190–191: *border ill.* Karen Blessen; *photo* Matt Heron Black Star. 192–193: Lawrence Migdale/Stock, Boston. 194–195: *border ill.* Karen Blessen; *photo* SuperStock. 196–197: *ill.* Alex Boies; *photo* Robert Daemmrich for SBG. 198–199: *bkgd.* W. Cody/Westlight; *inset* From *Mattie Lou O' Kelley: Folk Artist.* Copyright © 1989 by Mattie Lou O'Kelley. By permission of Little, Brown & Co. 200–201: *border ill.* Jackie Besteman; Howard Levy. 202–203: The Granger Collection. 204–205: *border ill.* Jackie Besteman. 205: Scala/Art Resource, New York. 206–207: *border ill.* Jackie Besteman; *photograph* SuperStock. 208–209: Karen Blessen. 210–211: *border ill.* Karen Blessen 210: Grant Heilman Photography. 211: *t.* SuperStock; *b.l., b.r.* Grant Heilman Photography. 212–213: *border ill.* Karen Blessen; *ill.* Kevin Short. 214–215: Francisco Mora. 216–219: Andrea Eberbach. 220–221: Stamps courtesy of Phoenix Stamp House. 224–225: Jason Laure. 227: Robert Fried/DDB Stock. 228: DUFY, Raoul. French. *The United Nations,* 1952. UNICEF Greeting Card Div., courtesy of UNICEF. 230–253 : Paulette Bogan. 254: Christopher Moroney. 256: Merlin D. Tuttle/Bat Conservation International, Inc. 257: Shelley Matheis. 258–259: John Lawlor/Tony Stone Images, New York. 260: Stock Imagery. 261: Kristine Bollinger. 262: British Library, London. The Bridgeman Art Library, England. 264: Randy Verougstraete. 265: Ron DuBuque. 266: SuperStock. 268: Brett, John. *Cardigan Bay.* Roy Miles Gallery, LONDON. Photograph: The Bridgeman Art Library, England. 270: JoAnn Adinolfi. 271: Anon. *The Musicians.* Hermitage, St. Petersburg/The Bridgeman Art Library, England. 271: Karen Blessen. 273: Kente Cloth courtesy of Riverstone, Morristown, NJ. 274–275: Stuart Simons. 277: Christopher Harris/Globe Photos. 278: SuperStock. 279: JoAnn Adinolfi. 280: Bruno De Hogues/Tony Stone Images, New York. 281: *ill.* Karen Blessen. 282: David Stocklein/The Stock Market. 283: Ken Spengler. 284: Eldon Doty. 285: *border ill.* Ron DuBuque; *photo* © Francois Gohier/Photo Researchers, Inc. 286–287: Graeme Norways/Tony Stone Images, New York. 289: Tony Stone Images, New York. 291: Jeff White. 292–293: Kathleen Kinkoph. 294–295: Thomas Hart. 296: Larry Lefever/Grant Heilman Photography. 298–299: Victor Vaccaro. 300–301: *border ill.* Kristine Bollinger; *photo* Jerry Jones for SBG. 302: Don Weller. 304–305: *ill.* Susan Todd. 304: Chad Ehlers/Tony Stone Images, New York. 305: David Tomlinson/Tony Stone Images, New York. 306–307: *ill.* Kristine Bollinger; *photos* The Granger Collection. 308–309: *ill.* Jackie Besteman; *photo* The Granger Collection. 310: *ill.* Karen Blessen: The Granger Collection. 311: *ill.* Karen Blessen; *photo* John Warden/Tony Stone Images, New York. 312: Liz Conrad. 314–315: Melanie Marden Parks.

Sound Bank Photos 330: *Charango*-Robert Houser for SBG. 332: *Mbira*-Mathers Museum. 333: *Siku*-Robert Houser for SBG. 334: *Tiple*-Robert Houser for SBG. 335: *Ughubu*-Mathers Museum.

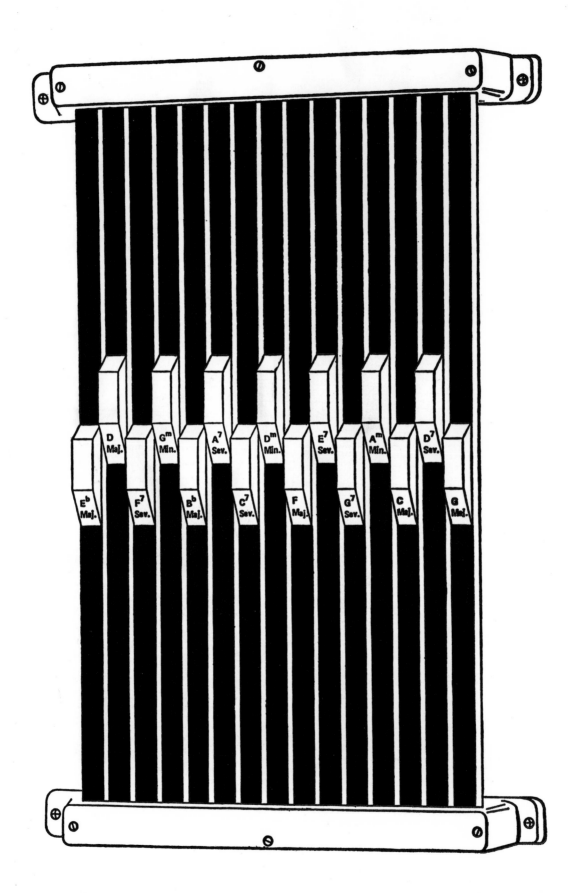